I0434344

TITANS OF SALES

Motivation Dies. Systems Don't.

CRAIG SCHNEIDER

Copyright © 2026 Craig Schneider

All rights reserved.

No part of this book may be reproduced in any form

without written permission from the publisher.

Published by Think Sales Press

ThinkSales.com

Library of Congress Control Number: 2026902948

ISBN: 979-8-9935131-0-2 (Paperback)

ISBN: 979-8-9935131-1-9 (eBook)

ISBN: 979-8-9935131-2-6 (Hardcover)

ISBN: 979-8-9935131-3-3 (Audiobook)

For Annie, who believed in the crazy dreams.

And to every Titan brave enough to chase theirs.

CONTENTS

PILLAR 5:   NEGOTIATION

PILLAR 6:   DISCIPLINE

PILLAR 7:   INNER CIRCLE

PILLAR 8:   UNBREAKABLE

The Making of a Titan

· · ·

I was sitting in my car in the driveway. Engine off. Hands still on the wheel.

Through the window, I could see the glow of the kitchen light. My wife was in there, probably cleaning up from dinner, keeping things running like she always did. Somewhere in the back of the house, my two little girls were getting ready for bed. They'd want a story. They'd want daddy to come tuck them in.

And I couldn't move.

I'd just gotten off the phone with my builder rep. One conversation. Three minutes. And everything changed.

The builder had decided to pull out of the neighborhood where I'd been working for months. Overnight. Without warning. A neighborhood I'd poured myself into. A neighborhood where I had pre-sold eight homes to eight families who trusted me.

Eight contracts. Gone.

Not because I did anything wrong. Not because the buyers backed out. Because someone in a corporate office somewhere made a business decision, and I was collateral damage.

I sat there doing the math I didn't want to do. To hit my goal for the month, to keep the mortgage paid, to keep food on the table, to not have to walk into that kitchen and tell my wife we were in trouble, I needed to close twelve deals in what was left of the month.

Twelve.

I'd never done that before. Most agents don't do twelve in a year.

The silence in that car was deafening. The kind where you can hear your own heartbeat. The kind where the voice in your head gets loud, telling you that you're not cut out for this, that you should've stayed in the Navy, that maybe you made a terrible mistake betting your family's future on commission checks.

I thought about my daughters. The way they looked at me like I could do anything. Fix anything. Handle anything. They didn't know that daddy was sitting in the driveway afraid to come inside. They didn't know that the man they believed in wasn't sure he believed in himself.

That's the loneliest feeling in the world. Being the one everyone's counting on and not knowing if you can deliver.

I sat there for a long time.

And then I got out of the car.

• • •

Before real estate, I spent ten years in the United States Navy.

Ten years of waking up before the sun. Ten years of being told that the standard isn't the standard. Exceeding it is. Ten years of learning that your feelings don't get a vote when the mission matters.

Towards the end of my honorable service, my job was to take raw recruits and turn them into something useful. To strip away the excuses. To build systems they could rely on when everything else was chaos. To show them that discipline wasn't punishment. It was freedom.

I thought I understood hard work when I left the service.

I was wrong.

Real estate humbled me in ways the military never did.

In the Navy, if you did the work, you got the result. The system was clear. Follow the process, execute the mission, go home. But in sales? You could do everything right and still lose. You could pour your soul into a client for three months and watch them sign with someone else. You could work eighty hours a week and have nothing to show for it. Or you could do everything right, build real relationships, earn real trust, and still have eight deals disappear overnight because of a decision you had no part in.

That randomness broke something in me. For a while, I thought I'd made a terrible mistake leaving the security of military life. I questioned everything.

But here's what I eventually learned: Sales isn't random. It just looks that way when you don't have a system.

• • •

That night, after I finally walked inside, after I tucked in my girls and pretended everything was fine, I made a decision.

I was going to treat real estate like a military operation. No more hoping. No more winging it. No more waiting for motivation to show up.

I built a system.

I reverse-engineered the math. How many conversations did I need to have to book one appointment? How many appointments to get one signed agreement? How many agreements to close one deal? And if I needed twelve deals in the time I had left, exactly how many calls did that mean today?

The number was brutal. But it was also clear. And clarity is everything when you're fighting for your life.

I stopped checking my feelings at the start of every day and started checking my metrics. I created scripts so I wouldn't have to think under pressure. I built follow-up sequences, so no lead ever fell through the cracks. I tracked everything. Calls, contacts, appointments, conversions. Because the scoreboard doesn't lie, even when your emotions do.

That month, I closed twelve deals.

That experience rewired me for life. Not because I discovered some hidden talent. Not because the universe rewarded my effort with a magic breakthrough. Because I learned something that most people in sales never learn: When you take emotion out of the equation and let the math lead, you can hit numbers you never thought possible.

• • •

That was years ago.

Since then, I've been responsible for over 2,500 real estate transactions. I've built and led a team that consistently ranks among the top in the region. I've trained hundreds of agents. Some came in knowing nothing. Some came in thinking they knew everything. The ones who listened, who implemented, who stayed disciplined? They changed their lives.

The ones who didn't? They're not in the business anymore.

This industry is unforgiving. More agents quit this business in five years than sailors who ring the bell at Navy SEAL training. Not because they're bad people. Not because they don't work hard. Because they never learn the difference between being busy and being productive. They never build systems that work when motivation doesn't. They never develop the mindset that turns rejection into fuel instead of poison.

I've watched it happen hundreds of times. Good people. Smart people. Hard-working people. Gone.

And I got tired of watching it.

But a few endure. A few decide they will not be average. They push through the rejection. They stop caring about the applause of vanity metrics and start caring about the math that feeds their family. They learn to outlast, to sharpen, to win.

Those are the Titans.

And here's the truth: Titans aren't born. They're built.

• • •

That's why I wrote this book.

Not to add another title to the shelf of motivational fluff that makes you feel good for an afternoon and changes nothing. Not to tell you that success is easy if you just believe hard enough. That's a lie, and you know it.

I wrote this because I wish someone had handed me this playbook when I was sitting in that driveway, afraid to walk into my own house. I wish someone had shown me the exact systems, scripts, and disciplines that separate the agents who survive from the ones who thrive. I wish someone had been honest with me about how hard it was going to be, and then shown me exactly how to win anyway.

No one did. So I had to figure it out the hard way. Twenty years of trial and error. Twenty years of testing what works and discarding what doesn't. Twenty years of refining the systems I now teach my team every single morning.

You're holding those twenty years in your hands.

Here's the truth most salespeople never learn:

Sales mastery isn't about what you do in the room. It's about who you've become before you walk in.

• • •

This book is for the agent who's been in the business three years and is still stuck at twelve deals. You know you're capable of more. You've had flashes of success. But something isn't clicking, and you can't figure out what.

It's for the new agent who doesn't want to spend five years learning lessons that could be learned in five months. If someone would just tell them the truth.

It's for the team leader who's tired of watching talented people wash out because they never learned the fundamentals that actually matter.

It's for anyone in sales, any industry, any product, who's ready to stop hoping and start building.

But let me be clear about who this book is not for.

It's not for the person looking for shortcuts. There are none.

It's not for the person who wants to be told they're already doing great. You might be. But if you were, you probably wouldn't need this book.

It's not for the person who's going to read this, nod along, and then do nothing different tomorrow. That person will fail, and no book can save them.

This book is for the person who's ready to do the work.

• • •

Here's what you'll find in these pages:

The mindset shifts that separate closers from complainers. Why most agents sabotage themselves before they ever pick up the phone, and how to stop.

The exact metrics that predict success. Not vanity numbers that make you feel productive. The real math. The numbers that feed your family.

Word-for-word scripts that I've tested over thousands of calls. What to say when they answer. What to say when they object. What to say when they're about to slip away.

The follow-up systems that turn cold leads into closed deals. Sometimes months after every other agent gave up.

Negotiation tactics that protect your client and your commission. How to hold the line when the other side pushes. How to win without making enemies.

The daily disciplines that compound over time. Small actions, repeated consistently, that create results most people think require talent or luck.

And the truth about building something bigger than yourself. How to lead a team. How to create systems that scale. How to build a legacy instead of just a job.

Every chapter stands alone. You can read them in order or jump to the section you need most. But I'll tell you this: the agents who get the most from this book are the ones who read it cover to cover, implement as they go, and then come back to it again and again.

• • •

I'm going to ask something of you before we begin.

Decide right now that you're going to do more than read this book. Decide that you're going to use it. That you're going to be uncomfortable. That you're going to try things that feel awkward at first. That you're going to track your numbers even when you don't want to know the truth. That you're going to make the calls even when your mind is making the best excuses.

Remember: Titans are built. One decision at a time. One discipline at a time. One day at a time.

The question isn't whether you have what it takes. You do. The question is whether you'll do what it takes.

I believe you will. That's why I wrote this for you.

Now let's get to work.

• • •

TITAN TRUTH

The distance between where you are and where you want to be isn't talent. It's discipline.

PILLAR I

MINDSET

CHAPTER I

The War Inside Your Head

Outperform Your Past Every Time

A man's own mind is the greatest battle he will face.

• • •

Your competition isn't other people.

Read that again.

The agent across town isn't your competition. The top producer on the leaderboard isn't your competition. The new team with the flashy marketing isn't your competition.

Your competition is ego. Self-doubt. Bad habits. Procrastination. Lack of discipline.

Compete against that.

Because here's what nobody tells you: The agent across town isn't stopping you from making calls. Your ego is. It whispers that you're above the grind, that cold calling is beneath someone of your experience. The new team down the street isn't stealing your clients. Your self-doubt is. It convinces you that you're not good enough to compete, so you don't even try. The market isn't killing your business. Your bad habits are. They let you hide in busy work while the hard things, the things that actually move the needle, sit undone.

Every Titan learns this truth early: The real battle isn't external. It's internal. Win there first, and everything else follows.

• • •

The Only Easy Day

In the Navy, we had a saying: The only easy day was yesterday.

It wasn't a complaint. It was a warning.

It meant that comfort is a trap. That the moment you think you've got it figured out is the moment you're most vulnerable. That yesterday's performance means nothing if you don't show up today.

Most salespeople never learn this. They hit a good month and coast. They close a big deal and relax. They build a little momentum and assume it will carry them forward.

It won't.

I've watched it happen so many times I've lost count. An agent has their best quarter ever. They feel invincible. They ease off the prospecting. They skip a few mornings of calls. They tell themselves they've earned a break.

Three months later, their pipeline is empty. The closings from their big quarter are done, but nothing new is coming behind them. They're scrambling, desperate, confused about how things fell apart so fast.

What went wrong was simple: They stopped fighting the real enemy.

The real enemy isn't the market. It isn't the competition. It isn't interest rates or inventory levels or whatever excuse is popular this month. The real enemy is the voice in your head that says you've done enough. That today's discipline can slide. That you can take your foot off the gas and coast for a while.

That voice will destroy you if you listen to it.

• • •

Control the Controllables

Here's a truth that will either free you or frustrate you, depending on how you receive it:

You cannot control outcomes. You can only control inputs.

You cannot control whether a buyer chooses you. You can control how fast you respond when they reach out. You cannot control whether a listing sells in week one. You can control how well you prepared the seller for reality. You cannot control market conditions. You can control how many conversations you have today.

Most agents pour their energy into things they can't control. They worry about the market. They complain about lead quality. They obsess over what competitors are doing. They spend hours on social media comparing themselves to people whose real numbers they don't even know.

All of that energy is wasted. Worse than wasted. It's destructive.

Titans focus only on what they can control: Their response. Their attitude. Their energy. Their boundaries. The way they speak. How they process setbacks. Who they spend time with. Their self-talk. Their discipline.

That's the list. Everything outside that list is noise.

When you stop bleeding energy into things you can't control and pour everything into the things you can, something shifts. You stop feeling like a victim of circumstance. You start feeling like a professional who creates results regardless of circumstance.

That shift changes everything.

● ● ●

The Weekly War

If your only real competitor is yourself, then you need a way to measure the battle.

Every week, my team fights the same war: Can we beat the version of ourselves from seven days ago?

Not can we beat the agent down the street. Not can we hit some arbitrary number that someone else set. Can we be better than we were last week?

The metrics are simple. How many calls did you make last week? Beat it. How many appointments did you book? Beat it. How many conversations turned into real opportunities? Beat it.

When you compete against yourself, there's no ceiling. There's no excuse. There's no one to blame. There's just the scoreboard from last week and a simple question: Do you have what it takes to improve on it?

This isn't motivation. It's math. And math doesn't care about your feelings.

• • •

The Agent Who Stopped Watching

A few years ago, I had an agent on my team who was stuck.

Not failing. Stuck. Twelve deals a year, every year. Enough to pay the bills. Not enough to build a life.

He had a wife, two kids, and a dream of something bigger. But every year, the dream stayed a dream. Same production. Same income. Same frustration.

His problem wasn't skill. He knew the scripts. He understood the market. When he actually got on the phone, he was solid.

His problem was that he spent more time watching other agents than working on himself.

Every team meeting, he'd ask what the top producers were doing. He'd study their marketing. He'd analyze their listings. He'd wonder out loud what secret they had that he was missing.

One day I sat him down.

"How many calls did you make last week?"

He didn't know.

"How many the week before?"

Didn't know that either.

"You're so busy watching everyone else that you don't even know what you're doing. For the next hundred days, I want you to ignore every other agent in this office. No leaderboard. No comparing. Just you against last week's version of you. Beat your own numbers. That's the only mission."

He pushed back. It felt too simple. He wanted a secret strategy, a hack, a shortcut.

There wasn't one. There never is.

But he committed. Week one: forty-two calls. Week two: fifty-three. Week three: sixty-one. By month three, he was averaging over a hundred calls a week and had booked more appointments in ninety days than he had in the entire previous year.

He didn't find a secret. He found focus. He stopped watching everyone else and started competing with the only person who actually mattered.

That agent doubled his income that year. His wife went back to school. They took their first real family vacation in five years. Not because the market changed. Not because he got lucky. Because he changed his mind about who the competition really was.

• • •

Action First

Most people wait to feel motivated before they act.

Titans know it works the other way around.

Action creates motivation. Not the other way around.

You don't wait until you feel like making calls. You make the first call, and somewhere around call three or four, you start to feel it. You don't wait until you're inspired to follow up with your database. You open the CRM, send the first message, and momentum builds from there.

The amateur waits for motivation to strike. The professional shows up and does the work whether motivation is there or not. And here's what the professional discovers: motivation almost always shows up once you start moving.

This is why discipline beats desire. Desire fluctuates. Discipline doesn't. Desire depends on how you feel. Discipline depends on what you've committed to.

Some mornings you'll wake up fired up, ready to conquer. Ride that wave. But most mornings? You'll wake up tired. Distracted. Full of reasons why today should be the exception.

Those are the days that define you.

Those are the days when Titans separate from everyone else.

Default to discipline. If it's important, don't wait to feel ready. Just start.

• • •

The Story You Tell Yourself

Every person carries a story in their head. A story about who they are, what they're capable of, what they deserve.

Some agents carry a story that says: I'm not a natural salesperson. I'm not good on the phone. I don't have the right connections. I'm not aggressive enough for this business.

And every day, they prove themselves right.

Other agents carry a different story: I'm building something. I'm getting better every week. I have what it takes. The work I do today is creating the results I'll see tomorrow.

They prove themselves right too.

The story you tell yourself isn't just words. It's programming. It shapes what you attempt, how hard you push, and whether you persist when things get hard.

Titans carry a specific story: I am the kind of person who finds a way. Not the kind of person who finds an excuse.

When a deal falls apart, the amateur says: "See? I knew this would happen." The Titan says: "What can I learn, and how do I prevent it next time?"

When the market shifts, the amateur says: "There's nothing I can do." The Titan says: "How do I adapt faster than everyone else?"

When the phone feels heavy, the amateur says: "I'll start tomorrow." The Titan says: "This is exactly when I need to pick it up. This is where the gap widens."

Here's a truth that will save you years of frustration: No one is coming to rescue you. The only person who's going to show up and save your career is you. The sooner you accept that, the sooner you take complete ownership of your results, the sooner everything changes.

• • •

The Question

From this day forward, before every decision, every action, every moment where you're tempted to take the easy path, ask yourself one question:

Would a Titan do this?

Would a Titan skip the morning calls because they're tired? Would a Titan let that lead sit for three days without follow-up? Would a Titan blame the market instead of adapting to it? Would a Titan coast after one good month?

You already know the answers. You've always known.

The mindset advantage isn't complicated. It's a decision. A decision to hold yourself to a higher standard than anyone else would hold you. To compete against yourself instead of others. To focus on what you control and release what you don't. To take action before you feel ready. To tell yourself a story of strength instead of limitation.

Every chapter that follows builds on this foundation. The metrics, the scripts, the systems, the disciplines. None of it works without the right mindset. None of it matters if you're still fighting the wrong enemy.

But get this right, truly internalize it, and everything else becomes easier.

Not easy. Easier.

Because you'll finally have the one advantage that can't be copied, bought, or stolen.

The mind of a Titan.

...

TITAN TRUTH

The battlefield is between your ears. Win there first.

CHAPTER 2

The Day I Stopped Selling

From Transactions to Trust

Don't listen to respond. Listen to understand.

• • •

One decision changed my entire career.

Not a strategy. Not a script. Not a marketing hack. A decision.

I stopped selling.

I don't mean I stopped working. I don't mean I stopped closing transactions. I mean I stopped viewing every person who walked through my door as a target to be converted. I stopped treating conversations as opportunities to pitch. I stopped measuring success by how quickly I could get someone to sign.

Instead, I made a commitment: Build a relationship with every single person who comes through that door. Not just the ready buyers. Not just the big budgets. Everyone.

Listen to their actual needs. Become their advocate. Focus on helping, not closing.

Trust that if I did those things consistently, the rest would take care of itself.

It did.

• • •

Flipping the Order

Most agents have it backwards.

They chase the sale, hope it leads to a satisfied customer, hope that customer sends a referral. Maybe. Someday.

Titans flip the order.

Relationship first. Trust second. Sales and referrals pour in as a result.

When you lead with relationship, everything changes. You're not desperate. You're not pushing. You're not trying to convince anyone of anything. You're simply trying to understand another human being and figure out how to help them.

The person across from you can feel the difference.

They've met agents who were calculating commission before the handshake was over. They've endured pitches that had nothing to do with their actual situation. They've been sold to their entire lives.

They're exhausted by it.

Then they meet you. You're not selling. You're listening. You're asking questions. You're genuinely curious about what they need, what they fear, what they're hoping for.

That experience is so rare it's almost disorienting. People wait for the pitch. They brace for the pressure.

When it doesn't come, walls fall. Trust rises. A relationship begins.

• • •

The Advocate

There's a difference between a salesperson and an advocate.

A salesperson wants the transaction. An advocate wants the best outcome for the person in front of them, even if that outcome doesn't include a commission.

I've told people not to buy. I've told people to wait. I've told people the house they loved wasn't right for them, even when I knew they'd sign that day if I let them.

Every time, something interesting happened.

They trusted me more. Not less. More.

Because I'd proven I was in their corner. I wasn't another person trying to extract something from them. I was their advocate, protecting their interests even when it cost me.

You can't fake this. People smell fake from across the room. Either you genuinely care about the person sitting across from you, or you don't. No script will save you if you don't.

But if you do care, if you truly make the shift from salesperson to advocate, something remarkable happens.

You stop chasing business.

Business starts chasing you.

• • •

The Art of Listening

Most people don't listen. They wait to talk.

Watch two average salespeople with a prospect. While the prospect talks, the salesperson is already formulating a response. Thinking about what point to make next. What objection to preempt. What close to set up.

They hear words. They don't absorb meaning.

Titans listen differently.

When someone talks, a Titan is fully present. Not planning the next sentence. Not looking for an opening to jump in. Just absorbing. Understanding. Paying attention to what's said and what's left unsaid.

This kind of listening is rare. Because it's rare, it's powerful.

When someone feels truly heard, they open up. They share things they haven't told other agents. Real fears. Real motivations. The real situation. That information is gold. It tells you exactly how to help. Exactly what they need to hear to move forward with confidence.

Here's the irony: The agent who talks less closes more. Because they know things the talkative agent never learned.

• • •

The Builder

Years ago, a builder called me. He was interviewing agents to represent a new development. Three finalists. Significant opportunity.

I knew what the other agents would do. Polished presentations. Stats. Awards. Testimonials. They'd walk in to impress.

I walked in with a legal pad and one question.

"What's your biggest headache right now?"

He paused. Studied me. No one had ever asked him that.

Then he started talking.

Thirty minutes. Problems with his current agent. Frustrations with sales pace. Investor pressure. Market concerns. I barely spoke. Took notes. Asked follow-up questions to make sure I understood.

When he finished, he looked at me.

"You're hired."

Not one slide. No track record mentioned. Nothing pitched.

But I'd done something the others hadn't. I'd listened. I'd made him feel understood. I'd shown him I cared more about his problems than my presentation.

That relationship lasted years. It led to opportunities I never could have imagined. All because I showed up to listen, not to impress.

• • •

The Family

A family came to me after a year of "just looking." Multiple agents. Dozens of homes toured. No commitment.

Other agents had tried urgency. Pressure. Clever objection handling.

I asked one question.

"What's really holding you back?"

Then I stopped talking.

Twenty minutes. Everything came out. Fear about schools in affordable neighborhoods. Worry about overpaying in a shifting market. Guilt about moving kids away from friends. Stress about actually qualifying for what they wanted.

None of this had surfaced with other agents. No one had asked. Everyone was too busy selling to listen.

I didn't pitch. Didn't pressure. Took their concerns one by one. Connected them with a lender for clarity on qualification. Pulled school ratings for every neighborhood in budget. Helped them see the move might actually improve their kids' situation.

Three weeks later, they called.

"We're ready."

I didn't close them. I advocated for them. Solved their actual problems instead of bulldozing through objections.

Four referrals since. All because I stopped selling long enough to actually help.

• • •

The Compound Effect

Here's what happens when you make this shift:

At first, not much. You're building relationships, but the payoff isn't immediate. You might feel like you're falling behind agents who push harder, close faster, grind through objections.

Ignore that feeling. Trust compounds.

Six months in, calls start coming from people you helped but didn't close. They're ready now. Or they know someone who is.

One year in, referrals arrive regularly. Your reputation is spreading.

Two years in, your phone rings with opportunities you didn't create. People you've never met call because their cousin said you're the only agent they'd ever trust.

Three years in, your business transforms. You're not chasing anymore. Not desperate for the next lead. Past relationships feed future business. Trust pays dividends you never could have earned through tactics alone.

This is the compound effect of trust. Slow at first. Then unstoppable.

Scripts get stale. Markets shift. Competitors copy your marketing.

Trust never expires. Trust is the one asset that appreciates, can't be copied, and compounds forever.

• • •

Your Choice

Two paths.

Path one: Keep doing what most agents do. Chase transactions. Push for closes. Measure success by signatures collected today. This path produces results at first. But you'll grind forever, always chasing the next deal, always starting from zero.

Path two: Make the decision I made. Stop selling. Build relationships with every person who walks through your door. Listen to their actual needs. Become their advocate. Focus on helping, not closing. This path is slower at first. But it compounds. Every relationship becomes an asset. Every person you help becomes a source of future business.

Over time, you stop chasing.

Business chases you.

I made my choice years ago. It changed my career. Changed my income. Changed how I feel about my work every single day.

Now it's your turn.

Stop selling. Start serving.

Trust the process.

The sales will follow.

They always do.

• • •

TITAN TRUTH

Lead with serving and you will never have to sell again.

CHAPTER 3

The Hunger Factor

Operating Beyond Your Limits

Fat dogs don't hunt.

• • •

That's the truth nobody wants to hear.

The agent who's comfortable, who's gotten a little soft, who doesn't need the next deal to survive? They stop doing the hard things. They skip the calls. They coast on past success. They tell themselves they've earned a break.

And slowly, quietly, their career starts dying.

Meanwhile, the hungry agent is still grinding. Still calling. Still pushing. Not because they're a masochist. Because they understand something the comfortable agent forgot: hunger is the fuel. Without it, nothing works. The scripts don't get practiced. The follow-ups don't get made. The uncomfortable conversations don't happen.

Successful people are hungry. Unsuccessful people are full.

That's not a judgment. It's just physics.

Titans know this. So they protect their hunger like their life depends on it. They never let themselves get full. They stay hungry on purpose, because they know the moment they stop being hungry is the moment they start getting passed.

• • •

Hunger Beats Talent

Talent is overrated.

I've watched naturally gifted agents wash out while average ones built empires. The difference was never ability. It was appetite.

The talented agent coasts. Relies on charm. Leans on natural communication skills. Waits for deals to fall in their lap. When things get hard, they don't know how to grind because they've never had to.

The hungry agent works. Studies when no one's watching. Practices scripts in the mirror. Makes the extra calls. Asks for feedback and actually implements it. Doesn't assume they'll figure it out. Fights to figure it out.

Same obstacle hits both agents. The talented one gets frustrated. Why isn't this working? The hungry one gets curious. What do I need to learn to break through?

Give me a hungry agent over a talented one every time. Hunger develops talent. Talent without hunger just wastes potential.

• • •

The Rookie

A new agent joined my team a few years back. No connections. No sphere of influence. No experience. By every traditional measure, he should have struggled for years before gaining traction.

He didn't.

What he lacked in experience, he made up for in hunger. Showed up first. Left last. Sat in on every training, even the ones that weren't required. Shadowed veteran agents. Asked so many questions they started hiding from him. Recorded his own calls, listened back, critiqued himself harder than any coach would.

He didn't just want to succeed. He needed to. You could see it in his eyes. Failure wasn't an option he was willing to consider.

By the end of year one, he wasn't the rookie anymore. He was outproducing agents who'd been in the business a decade. Not because he was more talented. Because he was hungrier. He wanted it more, so he worked for it more, so he got it.

That's the formula. No shortcut around it.

• • •

The Slow Death

Comfort doesn't kill you fast. It kills you slow.

I watched it happen to an agent who had everything going for him. Best listings in the office. Biggest commissions. All the recognition. He'd built something real.

Then he got full.

Stopped prospecting because he didn't think he needed to. Stopped learning because he thought he knew enough. Stopped pushing because pushing felt unnecessary when things were going well.

Within two years, he was irrelevant. Newer agents, hungrier agents, passed him like he was standing still. The market didn't care about his past success. It only cared about who was producing now.

And he wasn't.

Hunger is perishable. The moment you stop feeding it, it starts dying. Once it's dead, getting it back is ten times harder than keeping it alive in the first place.

Titans guard against comfort like a disease. The moment things feel easy, they know they're in danger. Raise the standard. Set a bigger goal. Find a new challenge. Whatever it takes to keep the hunger alive.

• • •

The Four Zones

There's a map that explains why most agents stay stuck.

Picture four concentric circles.

The center is the Comfort Zone. Feels safe. You're in control. Nothing challenges you. Most agents live here their entire careers, wondering why nothing changes.

Next ring out is the Fear Zone. This is where resistance lives. Lack of confidence. Excuses. Concern about what others think. Most agents hit this zone and retreat back to comfort. The fear feels like a wall, so they treat it like one.

But it's not a wall. It's a door.

Push through fear and you enter the Learning Zone. New skills. Real challenges. Problems to solve. It's uncomfortable, but you're growing.

Keep pushing and you reach the outer ring: the Growth Zone. Purpose. Goals achieved. The person you were always capable of becoming.

Most agents never make it past the Fear Zone. Not because they can't. Because they won't. They feel discomfort and assume it means stop.

Titans feel discomfort and know it means go.

• • •

The Edge

Growth doesn't happen in comfort. It happens at capacity's edge.

The bodybuilder doesn't grow lifting comfortable weight. They grow straining under the last rep. The runner doesn't build endurance jogging the same three miles. They build it running until their lungs burn.

Sales works the same way.

You don't grow staying where you are. You grow testing your limits. More calls. Tougher objections. Bigger goals. Harder conversations. Titans don't avoid these edges. They seek them.

Think about your first cold call. Every dial felt terrifying. After ten calls, palms sweating. After twenty, you thought you couldn't continue.

By your hundredth call? Fear was gone.

What changed? Not the calls. You. Your capacity expanded because you pushed past what felt possible.

Same principle applies to everything. Presentations. Negotiations. Follow-ups. What feels extreme today becomes baseline tomorrow. But only if you push through.

• • •

Breaking the Ceiling

Every agent has an invisible ceiling. The limit of what they believe they can handle. Most never test it, so it stays low.

I coached an agent who swore she couldn't make more than forty calls a day. Tried before. Always burned out. Forty was her ceiling.

I challenged her. Fifty calls a day for one week. Just five days.

First two days were ugly. Exhausted. Frustrated. Ready to quit. Day three, something shifted. Found a rhythm. Day four, hit fifty-two without realizing it. Day five, fifty-five.

Next week, she went back to her "normal" forty calls.

Her reaction? "This feels easy now."

That's the power of operating beyond your limits. Once you stretch, your old ceiling shatters. What felt impossible becomes baseline.

The ceiling was never real. It was psychological. Once you prove you can go beyond it, your belief system permanently expands.

• • •

The Recovery Principle

Operating at the edge doesn't mean burning out. There's a difference between pushing your limits and destroying yourself.

The formula: stress plus recovery equals growth.

Like muscles, performance grows when you alternate strain and rest. Push to the edge. Recover. Reflect. Recharge. Push again.

Without recovery, you break. Without stress, you stagnate. Balance the two and you become unstoppable.

Titans are strategic about intensity. They know when to pour everything in and when to step back. They schedule recovery the same way they schedule prospecting. Both are essential.

The goal isn't grinding until you collapse. The goal is expanding capacity over time. Sustainable intensity beats unsustainable heroics.

• • •

Feeding the Fire

Hunger doesn't maintain itself. You have to feed it.

The moment you achieve a goal, set another. Don't linger in celebration. Acknowledge the win, then ask: What's next?

Surround yourself with people ahead of you. Hunger thrives on proximity to greatness. If you're the most successful person in your circle, find a new circle.

Keep score. Track progress publicly. A visible scoreboard stokes hunger in ways private goals never can. When your numbers are exposed, you fight harder.

Stay uncomfortable. The moment things feel easy, find a new challenge. Take on something that scares you. Comfort kills hunger. Fear feeds it.

Remember why you started. When the grind gets heavy, reconnect with your original motivation. The house you want. The life you're building. The people depending on you. Let those images pull you forward when discipline alone isn't enough.

• • •

The Choice

Every day, you choose.

Comfort or growth. Safety or expansion. The easy path or the one that makes you better.

Hunger isn't something you have. It's something you choose. You choose it when you make the call you don't feel like making. When you study instead of scroll. When you stay late to finish what you started. When you refuse to settle for what you've already achieved.

The agents who dominate aren't the ones born with more talent or better circumstances. They're the ones who chose hunger when everyone else chose comfort. Who pushed past the fear zone when everyone else retreated.

That choice is available to you right now.

Today... What will you choose?

• • •

TITAN TRUTH

The hungry always eat.

PILLAR 2

METRICS

CHAPTER 4

The Law of 100

The Activity Standard That Guarantees Results

You can't cheat time. You can only invest it or waste it.

• • •

One week.

That's how long most agents give a strategy before they declare it dead.

They try calling expired listings for a week. Face rejection. Quit. Move to circle prospecting. Try that for a few days. Feels hard. Quit. Try FSBOs. Farming. Social media. Paid ads. Whatever the broker is pushing this month.

A year later, they've sampled everything and mastered nothing. They've given each strategy a week or two, never long enough to learn anything real.

They're exhausted. Frustrated. Convinced nothing works.

Meanwhile, an agent across town picked one strategy and committed to it for one hundred days. Didn't quit when it got hard. Didn't pivot when rejection stung. Showed up every single day, did the work, let the patterns emerge.

Now they're closing deals while the first agent is still shopping for magic.

This is the Law of 100. Not one hundred attempts. One hundred days.

• • •

Why Days

You can cram reps. You can't cram days.

An agent can make a hundred calls in two days when they're fired up. Grind through a burst of activity on pure adrenaline. But that's not where mastery lives. That's not where identity gets forged.

Mastery lives in consistency. Showing up on day fourteen when the excitement has faded. Showing up on day thirty-seven when you'd rather do anything else. Showing up on day sixty-two when results still haven't appeared.

One hundred days can't be gamed. Can't be shortcut. Can't be crammed into a motivated weekend.

You have to earn it. One day at a time.

That's the point.

A week tells you nothing. A month gives mixed signals. But one hundred days? That's when truth emerges. You know if the strategy works. You know what adjustments to make. You know if it's right for you.

More importantly, you know who you've become. Because one hundred days of showing up changes you.

· · ·

The Expired Commitment

An agent came to me frustrated. "Calling expired listings doesn't work. These people are angry and impossible."

How long did you try?

"About two weeks."

Two weeks. Fourteen days. And she was ready to bury the entire strategy.

I challenged her. Call expireds every single day for one hundred days. Same time. Same routine. No exceptions. Then tell me it doesn't work.

She pushed back. She'd seen enough.

No. You've seen fourteen days of discomfort. That's not data. That's feelings. Give it one hundred days. Then you'll have data.

She committed. Reluctantly.

First two weeks were brutal. Same rejection she'd faced before. But she kept showing up. By day thirty, she'd refined her opening. Conversations lasted longer. By day fifty, patterns emerged in the objections. She built responses for the common ones. By day seventy, she wasn't dreading the calls anymore. By day one hundred, she had seven listing appointments from expireds alone.

Same strategy she was ready to abandon at fourteen days.

Seven appointments at one hundred.

The strategy worked. She just hadn't given it enough days to prove it.

• • •

The Reset Trap

Every time you quit before one hundred, you reset to zero.

Think about what that means.

Three weeks of expired calls. Quit. Zero. Two weeks of FSBOs. Quit. Zero. Ten days of farming. Quit. Zero.

Forty-five days invested across three strategies. Nothing mastered. No real knowledge gained. No closer to clarity than when you started.

The agent who committed one hundred days to one strategy? They've got real knowledge. Real skill. Real confidence. They know what works and what doesn't. They've built momentum that compounds.

Same total time. Completely different results.

The reset trap is why agents stay stuck for years. They keep starting over. Never push through the hard middle to reach the clarity waiting on the other side.

Don't reset. Commit.

• • •

Fine-Tune, Don't Quit

The Law of 100 doesn't mean you can't improve until day one hundred.

It means you don't abandon the strategy until you've given it the full hundred days. You don't declare it broken. You don't chase something shinier.

But you absolutely adjust along the way.

The agent calling expireds noticed her opening wasn't landing. Tweaked it at day twenty-five. That's not quitting. That's improving. She noticed morning calls outperformed afternoons. Adjusted her schedule at day forty. That's not abandoning the strategy. That's optimizing it.

Fine-tuning is adjusting within the system. Quitting is abandoning the system before you understand it.

Titans fine-tune constantly. Never stop improving. But they earn that right by staying committed to the days. They don't blow up the whole approach because week two was hard.

Push through. Gather data. Adjust with precision.

• • •

The Veteran's 100

The Law of 100 isn't just for new agents. It works for veterans who've lost their way.

A seasoned agent came to me after a brutal year. Production down. Confidence gone. He wanted to reinvent everything. New branding. New niche. Blow it all up.

I gave him a different assignment.

One handwritten note to a past client every day for one hundred days. No reinvention. No new system. Just one note. Every day. One hundred days.

By day twelve, he hated it. Felt pointless. By day thirty, routine. By day fifty, old clients were responding. By day one hundred, he'd reignited relationships that turned into nine referrals and four closed transactions.

He didn't need reinvention. He needed consistency. The fundamentals he'd abandoned were still there, waiting for him to recommit.

Sometimes the answer isn't a new strategy. It's one hundred days of an old one you stopped showing up for.

• • •

Identity Through Days

Something shifts around day sixty or seventy.

You stop being someone who's "trying" the strategy. You become someone who does the strategy.

You're no longer experimenting with prospecting. You're a prospector. No longer testing a follow-up routine. You're someone who follows up. Every day. Without question.

It's just who you are now.

That identity shift is the hidden power of one hundred days. It doesn't just build skill. It builds you.

The agent who sees themselves as "someone who shows up every day" will always outperform the agent "trying to be more consistent." Same goal. Different identity. Different results.

One hundred days forges that identity. Day by day. Showing up when you don't feel like it. Doing the work when no one's watching. Proving to yourself that you honor your commitments.

By day one hundred, it's no longer a challenge.

It's just who you are.

· · ·

The Commitment

Here's what I'm asking:

Pick one strategy. One system. One daily discipline.

Commit to it for one hundred days.

Not one hundred attempts you can cram into a burst of motivation. One hundred days. One hundred times showing up. One hundred opportunities to learn, adjust, and grow.

Don't declare it broken at day fourteen. Don't abandon it at day thirty. Don't chase the next shiny object when you haven't finished what you started.

Give it the full hundred.

By day one hundred, you'll know. You'll have real data, not feelings. You'll have refined your approach through daily practice. You'll have become someone different than you were on day one.

That's the promise of the Law of 100.

Not just results.

Transformation.

• • •

TITAN TRUTH

Only the 100 know.

CHAPTER 5

The Scoreboard That Doesn't Lie

How Titans of Sales Use Numbers to Win

Numbers don't lie. But they can deceive you.

• • •

I watched a sales team celebrate like they'd won the championship.

Social media likes up. Website traffic climbing. Email open rates doubled. Charts looked beautiful. High-fives all around.

One problem: Pipeline was empty. No appointments. No contracts. No closings on the horizon.

One quarter later, half that team was gone.

They'd been celebrating the wrong numbers. Tracking the wrong scoreboard. Watching the wrong game while their business quietly starved.

The wrong metrics don't just distract you. They destroy you.

Titans know the difference. They track what matters, ignore what doesn't, and never confuse activity with results.

• • •

Vanity vs. Value

Two kinds of metrics in sales.

Vanity metrics feel good. Look impressive in a meeting. Make you think something is happening. Likes. Shares. Website visits. Email opens. Total dials without connects.

Value metrics feed your family. Measure what actually produces revenue. Conversations. Appointments. Presentations. Contracts signed. Referrals generated.

Vanity lives at the surface. Value digs down to the only thing that matters: money in your account.

Most agents track vanity. They know their follower count but can't tell you their conversion rate. Know how many emails they sent but not how many appointments those emails produced.

They're measuring the dribble, not the score.

If it doesn't lead directly to a conversation, appointment, or closing, it's vanity. Track it if you want. Don't confuse it with progress.

• • •

Leading and Lagging

Beyond vanity and value, another distinction matters.

Lagging indicators are results. Closed sales. Commission checks. Revenue. Everyone wants these. But by the time you see them, they're already in the past. You can't control them directly.

Leading indicators are inputs. Calls made. Conversations had. Appointments booked. Presentations delivered. These create lagging results. And these you can control.

Amateurs obsess over lagging indicators because they look impressive. Stare at the scoreboard wondering why the number isn't higher.

Titans focus relentlessly on leading indicators. That's where control lives.

You can't will a closing into existence. But you can control how many conversations you have this week. Conversations become appointments. Appointments become contracts. Contracts become closings.

Leading indicators today become lagging results tomorrow. Focus accordingly.

• • •

The Bridge

Between inputs and outcomes, there's a bridge: your ratios.

How many calls to get a conversation? How many conversations to book an appointment? How many appointments to sign a contract?

These ratios are your bridge metrics. They connect work to results. They tell you exactly where your leaks are.

Making calls but not booking appointments? Your call-to-appointment bridge is weak. Maybe your opening needs work. Maybe your ask needs to be stronger. Maybe you're calling at the wrong time.

Booking appointments but not signing contracts? Your presentation bridge is weak. Maybe you're not qualifying well enough. Maybe your value isn't landing. Maybe you're losing them on price.

Without bridge metrics, you're guessing. With them, you know exactly where to focus.

Titans pay close attention to their bridges. That's where the leverage is.

• • •

The 3M

Every month, I sit down with every agent on my team. Same meeting. Same structure. Same scoreboard.

We call it the 3M: Monthly Metrics Meeting.

One page. Seven sections. Everything that matters, nothing that doesn't.

Lead generation: Open houses. Networking events. New leads generated. The goal is simple. Sixty new leads per month from your own effort.

Database: How big is your list? How many new adds in the last thirty days? Are people properly tagged and tracked?

Follow-up: This is where most agents lie to themselves, so we dig deep. Total calls. Contacts made. Contact rate. Talk time. Response time to new leads. The goal is six hundred dials per month. Not contacts. Dials.

Appointments: How many set? How many kept? Big difference between booking an appointment and actually sitting across from someone.

Commitments: Buyer agreements signed. Listing agreements signed. The moments when someone says yes.

Contracts: Offers submitted. Offers accepted. Deals in progress.

Closings: Money in the door. What actually closed.

Seven sections. Nowhere to hide. You can't pretend you're working when the numbers say otherwise. Can't blame the market when the inputs aren't there.

The scoreboard tells the truth, even when you don't want to hear it.

• • •

Win the Week

Monthly tracking shows the big picture. But months are made of weeks. Weeks are made of days.

Every agent on my team tracks a weekly scoreboard. We call it Win the Week.

It's a point system. Every activity that matters has a value. Calls are two points each. Emails are five. Handwritten notes are five. Pop-bys are fifteen. Database adds are ten. Networking events are twenty.

Daily goal: one hundred fifty points. Weekly goal: nine hundred.

Hit your daily points, you win the day. Win four days, you win the week. Win three weeks, you win the month. Win eight months, you win the year.

That's the formula. Not complicated. Works because it takes the abstract idea of "working hard" and turns it into a system you can actually win.

Every day, agents know exactly where they stand. Not a feeling. A number. They either hit one fifty or they didn't. No gray area. No fooling yourself into thinking busy meant productive.

One rule makes the whole system work: Miss your accountability check-in, lose one hundred points. Skip one day of accountability and you've wiped out two-thirds of your effort.

Accountability without teeth is just suggestion. This system has teeth.

• • •

What Gets Measured

Old saying: What gets measured gets done.

True, but incomplete.

What gets measured gets done. What gets displayed gets owned. What gets reviewed gets improved.

Scoreboard has to be visible. Not buried in a CRM report. Not hidden in a spreadsheet you check once a month. On the wall. In your face. Updated daily.

Review has to be consistent. Every week, look at the numbers. Every month, sit down and assess. What worked? What didn't? What ratio improved? What broke?

Small course corrections create massive gains over time. But you can only correct if you're actually looking.

Most agents fly blind. Hope things are working. Assume they're on track. Only look at numbers when something feels wrong.

By then, it's usually too late.

• • •

The Crash

An agent came to me panicking. Great first quarter. Solid closings. Good income. Felt like she'd figured it out.

Second quarter? Nothing. Pipeline dried up. Phone stopped ringing. Couldn't understand what happened.

I asked to see her numbers.

She didn't have any.

No call tracking. No appointment tracking. No lead source tracking. She'd been winging it, riding momentum, assuming results would keep coming.

We reconstructed what we could. She'd stopped prospecting entirely after month two. Closings in quarter one came from activity she'd done months earlier. Once she stopped the inputs, took a few weeks for outputs to dry up. By the time she noticed, too late to fix quickly.

If she'd tracked weekly, she would have seen it in week one of quarter two. Calls down. Appointments down. Pipeline shrinking. Could have corrected immediately.

Instead, she flew blind until she crashed.

That's what happens when you don't measure. The crash always comes. Only question is whether you see it in time.

• • •

Simplicity Wins

Here's the trap: measuring too much.

I've seen agents with spreadsheets tracking fifty data points. Spend more time updating the tracker than doing the work. Complexity becomes an excuse to avoid the hard things.

Titans keep it simple. Five to seven key metrics. If it doesn't fit on one page, it doesn't belong in your daily focus.

Calls made. Conversations had. Appointments booked. Presentations delivered. Contracts signed.

That's the funnel. Track the funnel. Know your ratios at each stage. Identify where you're losing people and fix it.

Complexity is the enemy of execution.

Simple scoreboard. Consistent review. Ruthless honesty about what the numbers say.

• • •

The Truth

Numbers don't care about your excuses.

They don't adjust for how hard the market feels. Don't give you credit for being busy. Don't lie to make you feel better.

Numbers expose the truth about your effort, your effectiveness, and your future.

That truth can sting. Looking at a scoreboard that shows you're behind is never pleasant. Seeing your ratios exposed is humbling. Recognizing you're not working as hard as you thought? That hurts.

But the truth is always better than the alternative.

The agent who avoids the scoreboard lives in fantasy until reality crashes through. The agent who faces the numbers every day lives in reality and builds something sustainable.

Titans don't fear the truth. They hunt for it. Because once you see clearly, you can actually do something about it.

Track the right numbers.

Face the truth daily.

Let the scoreboard make you better.

• • •

TITAN TRUTH

Vanity feeds your ego. Metrics feed your family.

CHAPTER 6

The Compounding Effect of Consistency

"The real magic happens a decade, three decades later."

• • •

Nothing is happening.

That's what it feels like. You're making the calls. Sending the emails. Showing up to networking events. Following up with leads who seem permanently uninterested. Writing handwritten notes to people who never respond.

Week after week. Month after month. Nothing.

Then one Tuesday afternoon, your phone rings. Someone you met at an open house fourteen months ago. They're ready to buy. While you're on that call, an email arrives. A past client's coworker needs to sell. Before you can respond, a text comes through. Your mortgage partner has a referral. That night at dinner, your neighbor mentions their nephew is relocating to the area.

Four opportunities. One day. After months of silence.

This isn't luck. This is compounding.

Every consistent action you took during the quiet months was loading a spring. You couldn't see it tightening. You couldn't feel the tension building. All you felt was the effort of pushing against resistance that refused to budge.

But the spring was loading. And when it releases, it releases all at once.

• • •

The Invisible Work

Most agents quit during the loading phase.

They make calls for three weeks, book no appointments, and conclude that calling doesn't work. They send handwritten notes for a month, receive no responses, and decide notes are a waste of time. They attend networking events for six weeks, close no deals from those connections, and determine that networking isn't worth the effort.

What they fail to understand is that they quit during the work. The invisible work. The work that doesn't appear on any scoreboard. The work that looks exactly like failure until the moment it doesn't.

Compounding doesn't announce itself. There's no notification that reads: "Congratulations, you've completed 67% of the invisible work required for your breakthrough." There's only the grind. The same actions. The same discipline. Day after day, with no evidence that any of it matters. Until it does.

• • •

The Fire Hose

I watched it happen with two agents on my team.

For months, they executed the fundamentals. Consistent prospecting. Consistent follow-up. Consistent networking. Their activity numbers were solid, but their results were quiet. No dramatic wins. No breakthrough months. Just steady, invisible progress that didn't feel like progress at all.

Then one week, everything detonated. Two offers submitted. A new buyer signed. A listing appointment booked. Another referral arrived before the first one closed. It was, as one of them described it, "like drinking from a fire hose."

Nothing for months. Then everything at once.

That's not a fluke. That's the pattern. Consistent effort doesn't produce consistent results. It produces delayed results that arrive in clusters. The spring loads slowly, invisibly, painfully. Then it releases fast.

Agents who understand this don't panic during the quiet months. They know what's building. Agents who don't understand this quit right before the release.

• • •

The Every-Ten-Days Principle

Here's how you load the spring without burning out.

Every person in your database gets touched every ten days. Not randomly. Systematically. A rotation: email, then a hand-signed letter, then a phone call. Repeat.

Email on day one. Something of value. Market update. Neighborhood news. A resource they might actually use. Not a pitch. Value.

Hand-signed letter on day ten. Not typed with a signature slapped on. Handwritten. Personal. Something that proves you actually thought about them as a human being. These take time. That's precisely why they work. Anyone can blast an email. Few will invest the minutes to write by hand.

Phone call on day twenty. Quick check-in. How are things? Anything I can help with? Keep it short. Keep it genuine. Keep it consistent.

Then start over.

This system isn't complicated. It's also not easy. The discipline required to maintain this rotation across your entire database, month after month, year after year, is exactly what separates agents who compound from agents who plateau.

Every touch is a deposit. The account doesn't show growth for a while. But the balance is building. And when someone in that database is ready to move, your name is the only one they remember.

• • •

The Layered Approach

One channel isn't enough.

Email alone gets lost in the noise. Phone calls alone feel intrusive. Letters alone seem random. But layer them together, phone plus email plus handwritten card plus social media, and something different happens.

They see your email Tuesday. Your name barely registers. They receive your letter Friday. Now they're curious. You comment on their social media post the following week. Now you're on their radar. Your call the week after doesn't feel cold. It feels like the natural continuation of an ongoing relationship.

Each layer reinforces the others. Each touch makes the next touch more effective. The compound effect isn't just about time. It's about layers building on layers until your presence in their life feels inevitable.

One email is noise. Six months of layered communication is a relationship.

• • •

The Card That Lived

Digital communication disappears. Physical mail survives.

I've had clients tell me they still have a card I sent them five years ago. Stuck on their refrigerator. Tucked in a drawer they open regularly. Sitting on a desk where they see it every morning. Five years later, my name is still occupying space in their daily life.

Emails get deleted. Texts get buried. Phone calls fade from memory within hours. But a physical card, something they can touch and hold, takes up space in their world. It has weight. It has presence. It exists.

Nobody's getting a mailbox full of handwritten cards. That's what makes yours remarkable. In a world drowning in digital noise, physical presence compounds differently. It lingers. It accumulates. It builds emotional associations that pure convenience can never create.

An email says you had thirty seconds. A handwritten card says you made time. That difference compounds over years into a relationship your competitors cannot replicate.

• • •

The Decades Payoff

Here's what most agents never stick around long enough to see.

Help someone buy their first home today. Stay in touch. Consistently. Ten years later, they've built equity. They're ready to upgrade. That's transaction two.

Stay in touch. Fifteen years later, they're pulling equity to fund their kid's college tuition. They call you for guidance. You connect them with the right lender. They remember that.

Twenty years later, their daughter is getting married. Needs a place to live. Your name surfaces at the rehearsal dinner. Transaction three.

Twenty-five years later, they're downsizing. Empty nest. Ready to sell the family home you helped them purchase a quarter century ago. Transaction four. And their children are now starting families of their own.

One relationship. Maintained consistently. Four transactions minimum. Plus referrals along the way. Plus the next generation.

This is what compounding looks like over a career. Not this quarter's numbers. Not next year's goals. A business built on relationships that span decades. But only if you stay consistent. Only if you keep loading the spring even when you can't see the payoff.

• • •

The Little Things

Small consistent actions beat large sporadic efforts. Every single time.

Five calls a day, every day, beats fifty calls on Monday followed by nothing the rest of the week. Two handwritten notes daily beats twenty notes crammed into a single Saturday afternoon. One coffee meeting per week, fifty-two weeks straight, beats a networking blitz that flames out by February.

Consistency isn't about intensity. It's about inevitability. When you do something every single day, it stops being something you do. It becomes part of who you are. It no longer requires willpower. It becomes automatic. Sustainable. Permanent.

Those little things, the ones that feel too small to matter, are exactly what compound. One adjustment to your morning routine. One additional follow-up call. One extra note per day. None of it feels significant in the moment.

But those little things that make a difference? One little tweak can have monstrous results. Given enough time.

. . .

The Patience Tax

Compounding demands patience. That's the tax you pay for exponential returns.

Year one feels like pushing a boulder uphill. Maximum effort. Minimum visible progress. Your scoreboard looks nearly identical to agents doing half the work. That's demoralizing. It's supposed to be.

Year two, the boulder begins to move more easily. The relationships you cultivated in year one are starting to produce. The follow-up sequences are generating callbacks. The network you built is beginning to refer.

Year three, the boulder has momentum. You're no longer pushing. You're steering. Past clients call before you call them. Referrals arrive without prompting. Your reputation does work that once required grinding effort.

Year five, the boulder is rolling downhill. You're running to keep up. Business finds you. Opportunities compound on opportunities. The machine you constructed through consistent daily effort is now generating returns you never could have produced through hustle alone.

But you have to survive years one and two. You have to keep pushing when the scoreboard says you're losing. That's the tax. Most agents refuse to pay it. They want the results of year five with the patience of year one. It doesn't work that way.

. . .

The Choice

You can chase transactions or build compounding assets. You cannot do both.

Transaction chasers start over every month. Close a deal, scramble for the next one. Every January resets to zero. Five years in, they're grinding just as hard as year one. Often harder. The treadmill never stops because they never built anything underneath them.

Compounders build something that grows. Every relationship becomes an asset on the balance sheet. Every consistent touch adds to the account. Every year builds on the foundation of the last. Five years in, they're working smarter because their past efforts are generating present results.

Same industry. Same market. Same number of hours in the day. Radically different experience.

The transaction chaser burns out or quits. The compounder builds wealth and freedom.

The only question is which path you're willing to walk. And whether you have the patience to let compounding do its work.

. . .

Find the consistency in your business, and you'll find the success that comes from it.

Not overnight. Not in a week. Not in a quarter. But inevitably. Relentlessly. Unstoppably. Consistent effort applied over time produces results that no amount of sporadic intensity can match.

The spring is loading right now. Every call you make. Every note you write. Every relationship you nurture. Every follow-up you refuse to skip. It's all going somewhere, even when you can't see the destination.

Keep loading.

The release is coming.

• • •

TITAN TRUTH

Consistency loads the spring.

SCRIPTS

CHAPTER 7

Don't Get Bucked

Hook Them in 8 Seconds

"Under pressure, you don't rise to the occasion. You fall to your preparation."

• • •

Eight seconds.

That's how long a bull rider has to prove they belong. Eight seconds of controlled chaos, gripping with everything they have while a thousand pounds of fury tries to throw them into the dirt. Stay on for eight, and the ride counts. Get bucked before that, and nothing else matters. The form doesn't matter. The reputation doesn't matter. The potential doesn't matter. You're just another rider eating dust.

Sales works the same way.

When you pick up the phone, you have about eight seconds to earn the right to continue. Eight seconds before the other person's brain decides whether you're worth listening to or just another interruption to dismiss.

Eight seconds to prove you're different from the hundred other salespeople who wasted their time this month.

Most agents get bucked before they ever get started.

Titans stay on. And the ride that follows changes everything.

• • •

The Telemarketer Trap

You know the sound. The second you hear it, your finger moves toward the end call button.

Low energy. Monotone. Reading from a script they don't believe in. A slight hesitation that screams uncertainty. That split-second pause after you say hello where you can almost hear them scrambling for their next line.

That's the telemarketer sound. If your opening carries even a hint of it, you're done. Not in thirty seconds. Not after your pitch. Done before you finish your first sentence.

I listened to a call once from an agent who couldn't figure out why his prospecting wasn't producing. Within three words, I knew. His energy was flat. His tone apologized for existing. He sounded like someone who expected rejection, and his prospects were happy to deliver it.

The words were fine. The script was solid. But his delivery had the telemarketer sound, and no amount of perfect phrasing overcomes that. People don't hang up on scripts. They hang up on energy.

Your first eight seconds must sound like someone worth talking to. Confident. Clear. Unhurried. Someone who has something valuable to offer and knows it. The moment you sound like you're interrupting or apologizing, you've already been bucked.

• • •

Earning Time

Here's how the math works.

Your first eight seconds earn you two minutes. Your first two minutes earn you twenty. Your twenty minutes earn you the appointment.

Each stage is a gate. You don't get to skip ahead. You can't leap from eight seconds to the closing table. You earn your way through each gate, proving at every stage that you're worth more of their attention.

Your only job in the first eight seconds is to earn two minutes. That's it. Not to close. Not to pitch. Not to qualify. Just to be interesting enough, relevant enough, human enough to warrant two more minutes of their time.

• • •

The First Two Minutes

You've hooked them. They didn't hang up. Now what?

The next two minutes serve one purpose: building trust. Not pitching. Not selling. Not rattling off credentials or company awards. Building a human connection that makes them want to keep talking.

You do this by asking questions. Not qualification questions. Not "how many bedrooms are you looking for" questions. Questions that spark conversation. Questions that show genuine curiosity about their situation. Questions that let them talk while you listen.

"What's driving the timing for you?" "How long have you been thinking about this?" "What would make this move feel like a win for your family?"

These questions accomplish two things. First, they get the prospect talking about themselves, which people naturally enjoy. Second, they demonstrate that you're not another agent running through a script. You're someone who actually cares about understanding their situation before trying to solve it.

Your professionalism shows in how you ask. Your confidence shows in how you listen. Your value shows in the follow-up questions that prove you were paying attention.

Two minutes of genuine conversation builds more trust than twenty minutes of pitching ever could. Earn the trust first. The next gate opens.

• • •

The Twenty Minutes

You've earned their trust. They're still engaged. Now you have the runway to do what you called to do: lock down the appointment.

That's the whole reason for the call. Not to close a deal over the phone. Not to answer every question they might ever have. To get face-to-face, where real business happens.

During these twenty minutes, you're doing two things simultaneously. First, you're showing how you provide value. Not telling. Showing. Through the questions you ask, the insights you offer, the way you handle the conversation. They should be thinking, "This person actually knows what they're doing."

Second, you're quietly determining if this lead is a good fit for you. Not every prospect deserves your time. Not every inquiry becomes a client. During this conversation, you're listening for signals. Are they serious or just curious? Is the timeline real or imaginary? Do they have the capacity to move forward?

This is where you earn the right to qualify. Not in the first eight seconds. Not in the first two minutes. Here. After trust is established. After value is demonstrated. Now you can weave in the questions that help you determine if this is someone worth meeting.

The twenty minutes isn't about convincing them you're good enough. It's about both of you discovering if there's a fit. When there is, the appointment books itself.

• • •

The Hook

Every person you call has a radio station playing in their head. The call letters are WIIFM: What's In It For Me?

That station never turns off. While you're talking, they're scanning for relevance. Is this about me? Does this solve my problem? Is this worth my time? The moment the answer is no, they tune out. Doesn't matter if you keep talking. They're already gone.

Your first eight seconds must answer their station. Not your name. Not your company. Not your credentials. Their problem. Their desire. Their situation.

A weak opener sounds like this: "Hi, this is John with ABC Realty, and I was just calling to see if you might be thinking about buying or selling in the near future."

That opener is about John. John's company. John's agenda. There's nothing in it for the person on the other end. No hook. No curiosity sparked. Just another salesperson making another sales call. Click.

A strong opener flips the focus: "Hi, this is John with ABC Realty. Quick question: if a buyer offered you the right price for your home this spring, would you be open to hearing about it?"

Same person. Same company. Completely different response. Now there's a hook. Now there's curiosity. Now there's something in it for them. The question speaks to their opportunity, not John's agenda. That difference buys you two minutes.

· · ·

Commission Breath

People can smell desperation through the phone.

When you need the deal too much, it shows. Your voice tightens. Your energy shifts. You push too hard, agree too fast, accommodate too much. You have commission breath, and prospects recoil from it the same way they'd recoil from someone standing too close with actual bad breath.

Commission breath kills your first eight seconds before you even open your mouth. The prospect hears hunger, and not the good kind. Not the kind that drives excellence. The desperate kind. The kind that signals you need them more than they need you.

Titans approach every call from a position of value, not need. They're not calling because they need a commission. They're calling because they have something worth offering. That difference in energy changes everything.

Before you dial, check your energy. If desperation is driving the call, put the phone down. Reset. Remember what you actually bring to the table. Then call from that place. Confident. Valuable. Worth talking to. Commission breath gone.

● ● ●

The FSBO

For Sale By Owners get called by agents constantly. Twenty, thirty times a week sometimes. Every call sounds identical: "Hi, I noticed your home is for sale. Are you offering a commission if I bring a buyer?"

They've heard it so many times they can finish the sentence before you do. Their finger is already on the end call button. You're not a person to them. You're call number twenty-three this week, indistinguishable from the twenty-two before.

An agent on my team was struggling with FSBOs. Getting hung up on constantly. Ready to abandon the entire lead source.

We rewrote his opener: "Hi, I saw your home is listed for sale by owner. Quick question, if I could show you how to net the same amount or more without paying a traditional commission, would you be open to that conversation?"

Different hook. Different outcome. That opener bought him two minutes because it answered their radio station. FSBOs aren't trying to avoid commission for the fun of it. They're trying to net more. The opener spoke directly to what they actually wanted.

Two minutes became twenty. Twenty became listing appointments. Same agent. Same FSBOs. Different first eight seconds.

...

The 300-Person Standard

Here's the standard I hold my team to: I want you so confident in your opening that you'd deliver it in front of 300 industry experts without hesitation.

Not 300 strangers. 300 experts. People who know every trick, every technique, every weak opener they've ever heard. People who would catch you faking it. People who would know instantly if you didn't believe what you were saying.

That's the bar. If you can deliver your opener with that level of confidence, a single prospect on the phone is nothing. If you've practiced until you could perform in front of experts, the actual call feels easy.

Most agents practice until they can get the words right. Titans practice until they can't get the words wrong. There's a difference. Getting it right means you can do it when conditions are perfect. Can't get it wrong means you deliver it the same way whether you're fresh or exhausted, confident or nervous, on your first call or your fiftieth.

Your opening should be so ingrained that your brain doesn't have to think about it. That frees you to focus on what matters: listening, reading the response, adjusting in real time. You can't do any of that if you're still thinking about what to say next.

...

Your Brain Will Sabotage You

Here's something nobody tells you about phone prospecting: if you don't fully believe in what you're doing, your brain will actively sabotage your success.

You'll stumble on words you know perfectly well. You'll forget phrases you've said a hundred times. You'll hear yourself using weak language, qualifying statements, escape routes. "I was just wondering if maybe you might possibly be interested..."

That's not nerves. That's your subconscious protecting you from rejection by ensuring you never fully commit. If you don't really ask, you can't really be rejected. Your brain thinks it's helping. It's not.

The cure is belief. Genuine belief that what you're offering has value. Genuine belief that the person you're calling would benefit from talking to you. Genuine belief that you're not interrupting their day but offering them something worth their time.

When you believe that fully, your brain stops sabotaging. The words flow. The confidence shows. The first eight seconds land. Not because you tricked yourself into performing, but because you're telling the truth about what you offer.

· · ·

The Ride

The bull doesn't care about your feelings.

It doesn't care that you're tired or that your last three rides ended badly or that confidence isn't showing up today. The bull tries to throw you regardless. Your job is to be ready regardless.

Every call is a new ride. The prospect doesn't know about your previous calls. They don't know you've been rejected fifteen times today. They don't know you're doubting yourself. All they know is what they experience in the first eight seconds with you.

That's a gift. Every call is a fresh start. Every opener is a clean slate. The last call has no power over this one unless you hand it that power.

Ride each eight seconds like it's the only one that matters. Grip tight. Stay focused. Don't let the previous bucks affect your form.

Titans get bucked too. Everyone does. The difference is Titans climb back on immediately, reset their form, and ride the next eight seconds like the last one never happened.

· · ·

Eight seconds.

That's the window. That's where the ride is won or lost.

Master your first eight seconds, and you earn two minutes to build trust. Master your two minutes, and you earn twenty to demonstrate value and determine fit. Master your twenty, and you earn the appointment.

But it all starts with the first eight. Get bucked there, and nothing else happens. Stay on, and everything becomes possible.

Practice your opener until you could deliver it in front of 300 experts. Eliminate the telemarketer sound. Check your energy for commission breath. Hook with relevance, not credentials.

Ride the eight seconds like your career depends on it. Because it does.

• • •

TITAN TRUTH

Eight seconds. That's all you get.

CHAPTER 8

Every No is a Door

The Art and Science of Closing Resistance

"If you're getting bad responses, it's usually not the clients, it's the questions you're asking."

· · ·

The objection isn't the problem.

Most agents hear "no" and assume the conversation is over. They retreat. They apologize. They hang up convinced the prospect wasn't interested, the timing wasn't right, some people just can't be helped.

They're wrong.

An objection isn't a wall. It's a door with a lock on it. The prospect is telling you exactly what stands between them and yes. They're handing you the key. Most agents see the lock and walk away. Titans see the lock and figure out which key fits.

Every objection is information. Every hesitation reveals a fear. Every "I need to think about it" is a request for help they don't know how to ask for.

Master the objection, and you master the close.

• • •

The Real Problem

When objections keep coming, the instinct is to blame the prospects. They're not serious. They're not qualified. They're just kicking tires.

Sometimes that's true. Most of the time, the problem isn't them. It's you.

Specifically, the questions you're asking. Bad questions produce bad responses. Weak framing produces weak engagement. If every call ends with the same objection, that's not coincidence. That's a pattern. Patterns point to the source.

I've watched agents blame prospects for months before realizing their entire approach was triggering the resistance they kept encountering. They weren't unlucky. They were untrained.

Before you diagnose the prospect, diagnose yourself. What question led to that objection? What framing created that resistance? What could you have said differently? The agents who ask these questions improve. The agents who blame prospects stay stuck.

• • •

What They're Really Saying

Objections are never about the words on the surface.

When someone says "I need to think about it," they're not asking for time to contemplate. They're saying, "I'm afraid of making the wrong choice, and I don't trust this decision yet."

When they say "It's too expensive," they're not commenting on your price. They're saying, "I'm not convinced the value matches what you're asking."

When they say "I'm already working with someone," they're not necessarily loyal. They're saying, "I don't see a compelling reason to switch."

When they say "Call me later," they're saying, "I don't see urgency, and you haven't given me a reason to act now."

Every objection is a translation problem. The words they use aren't the message they're sending. Your job is to hear what's underneath. The fear. The hesitation. The unspoken question they're really asking.

Learn to translate, and objections stop being obstacles. They become roadmaps.

• • •

The Three Fears

At the core of every objection, you'll find one of three fears.

Fear of loss. "I don't want to waste money. I don't want to make a financial mistake. I don't want to end up worse than I started."

Fear of risk. "I don't want to make the wrong choice. I don't want to commit to something that fails. I don't want to feel stupid for trusting the wrong person."

Fear of judgment. "What will my spouse think? What will my friends say? What if everyone tells me I made a mistake?"

Three fears. That's it. Every hesitation you'll ever encounter traces back to one of these. Every "I need to think about it." Every "Let me talk to my spouse." Every "I'm not sure this is the right time." One of these three fears is driving it.

When clients feel safe from loss, confident in their choice, and protected from judgment, resistance dissolves. Your job isn't to argue past objections. It's to address the fears beneath them.

• • •

The Battle Plan

You don't walk into battle without a plan. You don't pick up the phone without knowing exactly how you'll handle the objections coming your way.

Because they are coming. Every call. Every prospect. Objections aren't surprises. They're certainties. The only question is whether you're prepared or scrambling when they arrive.

Titans build a battle plan. For every common objection, they have a response ready. Not a script recited robotically, but a framework internalized so deeply that the right words flow naturally.

"I need to think about it" has a response. "I'm already working with someone" has a response. "Call me later" has a response. "It's too expensive" has a response. Every objection you hear more than once deserves a tested, refined, practiced answer.

The battle plan isn't manipulation. It's preparation. When you know exactly how to handle resistance, you stop fearing it. When you stop fearing objections, you stop triggering more of them. Confidence is contagious. So is uncertainty.

Build your plan. Practice until it's automatic. Walk into every conversation knowing nothing they say can catch you off guard.

$$\bullet\ \bullet\ \bullet$$

The Overpriced Seller

An agent on my team sat across from a seller who refused to accept the suggested listing price.

"That's too low," the seller said. "My neighbor's house sold for more."

The easy response would have been to cave. Agree to the higher price. Get the listing signed and deal with consequences later. That's what average agents do. They avoid conflict, take the overpriced listing, then watch it sit on market for months.

Instead, the agent addressed the fear underneath. "I understand you want to maximize value. That's exactly what I want too. But here's what happens if we price too high: buyers skip your home. Days on market climb. The listing becomes stale. You end up reducing anyway, but now from a position of weakness."

Then the agent painted a different picture. "Here's what happens if we price strategically: we create competition. Multiple buyers see value. They bid against each other. The price goes up because demand drives it, not because we wished it higher."

The seller leaned in. Fear of loss addressed. Alternative made vivid. The listing went live at the strategic price. Multiple offers came in. Home sold over asking.

That's objection mastery. Not arguing. Not caving. Understanding the fear, addressing it directly, showing a better path forward.

• • •

The Confidence Play

One of the most counterintuitive objection handlers I've seen came from an agent on my team who was losing a prospect to the competition.

The prospect said, "I'm interviewing a few agents before I decide."

Most agents hear that and panic. They sell harder. They list credentials. They offer discounts. They do everything possible to prevent the prospect from talking to anyone else.

This agent did the opposite. "Good," she said. "You should interview other agents. I'd encourage you to talk to at least two or three more. Ask them the same questions you asked me. Compare their answers. Then decide."

The prospect was stunned. No agent had ever told them to interview the competition. The confidence was so unexpected, so different from the desperate pitches they'd heard, that it immediately elevated her above everyone else.

The prospect didn't interview anyone else. They signed that day.

Sometimes the best objection handler is radical confidence. When you truly believe in what you offer, you're not threatened by comparison. You welcome it. That energy communicates more than any script ever could.

• • •

The Power of Silence

When faced with an objection, most agents panic and fill the silence with words. More explaining. More justifying. More talking that sounds increasingly desperate with every sentence.

Titans use silence as a weapon.

Address the objection. Make your point. Then stop. Let the silence sit. Give the prospect space to process. Let them think. Let them feel. Let them reach their own conclusion without you filling every second with noise.

Silence is uncomfortable. That's what makes it powerful. Most people rush to fill it. Whoever speaks first after an objection is handled usually loses. If you've made a strong point, let it land. Don't dilute it with nervous chatter.

The prospect needs time to move from objection to agreement. That movement happens in silence, not in your continued talking. Trust the silence. It's working even when it feels awkward.

• • •

Pre-Handling

The best objection is the one that never gets raised.

Titans don't wait for objections to surface. They pre-handle them. Before the prospect voices the concern, the Titan has already addressed it.

If price will be a sticking point, explain the value before they ask about cost. If timing is an issue, establish urgency before they suggest waiting. If competition is a factor, differentiate before they mention other options.

Pre-handling isn't guessing. It's anticipating. After enough conversations, you know which objections are coming. You've heard them dozens of times. Hundreds maybe. Why wait for them to be raised when you can neutralize them before they form?

When you pre-handle effectively, prospects feel understood. They feel like you're reading their mind. They feel like you've done this before and know exactly what someone in their position would worry about. That builds trust faster than any response to an objection ever could.

• • •

Practice in Public

Here's what separates agents who plateau from agents who improve: make your calls in front of senior agents.

Most people practice in private. They role-play with themselves. They rehearse in the shower. They think about what they'll say while driving. All of that helps. None of it compares to performing in front of people who can give real feedback.

When you make calls in front of experienced agents, you get immediate coaching. "You hesitated after they said that." "Your energy dropped when they objected." "You missed an opportunity to reframe." Feedback you'd never catch on your own.

Yes, it's uncomfortable. Yes, it's vulnerable. Yes, your ego will resist. That's exactly why it works. Growth lives at the edge of comfort. If practicing in front of others feels scary, that's a sign you need to do it more, not less.

After every call, ask one question: "What could I have said better?" Then actually listen. The agents who seek feedback improve. The agents who avoid it stay average.

• • •

The Objection Journal

Titans keep a record of every objection they encounter.

Not in their head. On paper or in a document. Every objection. Every response attempted. What worked. What didn't. What to try differently next time.

Over time, this journal becomes a personal playbook. A collection of battle-tested responses refined through actual conversations. Not theory from a book. Not scripts someone else wrote. Your words, proven in the field, ready to deploy.

The best agents don't wing it. They document. They refine. They improve with every conversation. Every objection becomes a lesson. Every failure becomes a future win.

Start your journal today. Write down the last three objections you heard. Write down how you responded. Write down what you wish you'd said. That simple practice, repeated consistently, transforms your objection handling faster than any training course.

. . .

Objections aren't the end of the conversation. They're the beginning of the real one.

Every "no" contains information. Every hesitation reveals a fear. Every resistance points to what the prospect needs to hear before they can move forward.

Build your battle plan. Translate what they're really saying. Address the fears underneath. Pre-handle what you can predict. Use silence as a weapon. Practice in front of people who can make you better. Document everything.

Do this consistently, and objections stop being threats. They become the moments where average agents retreat and Titans advance.

Master the objection. Master the close.

• • •

TITAN TRUTH

Every no is a door. Find the key.

CHAPTER 9

Storyselling

Tales That Make Sales

"Facts tell. Stories sell."

• • •

Nobody remembers your statistics.

They don't remember your market analysis. They don't remember the comparable sales you pulled or the absorption rate you quoted or the precise percentage by which homes in the area appreciated last quarter. They nodded while you said it. They forgot it before they stood up from the table.

But they remember the story about the couple who waited too long and lost their dream home. They remember the family who priced too high and watched their listing go stale. They remember the first-time buyer who almost walked away but didn't, and how it changed everything.

Stories stick. Data slides off.

This isn't a weakness in human cognition. It's how we're wired. For a hundred thousand years, humans passed down survival information through stories told around fires. Our brains evolved to encode narratives, to remember characters and consequences, to learn from other people's experiences without having to live them ourselves.

Titans understand this. They don't just sell. They storysell.

• • •

The Triangle Bottle

Years ago, I learned about a Scottish whisky with an unusual bottle. Triangular. Distinctive. The kind of shape you notice on a shelf.

Someone told me the story behind it. The founder designed that triangle shape to represent the three essential elements of his whisky: water, barley, and the air of the Scottish Highlands. Earth, grain, and atmosphere, unified in one vessel. The shape wasn't an accident or a marketing gimmick. It was a philosophy made physical.

Years later, someone else told me a different story. The founder liked to keep a bottle under his bed for a nip before sleep. Round bottles rolled. Every time he reached for it in the dark, it would roll away and clatter across the floor, waking his wife. So he designed a bottle that wouldn't roll. Three flat sides. Problem solved.

I have no idea which story is true. Maybe neither. Maybe both. Doesn't matter.

Because now you'll never forget that bottle.

That's what stories do. The liquid inside didn't change based on which origin story you heard. But your experience of it did. The bottle went from an interesting shape to a vessel with meaning, character, history. Real or embellished, the stories transformed how you relate to the product.

That's storyselling. You don't change what you're offering. You change how the client experiences what you're offering.

· · ·

Why Stories Bypass Resistance

When you present facts, the client's brain goes into evaluation mode. Is this true? Is this relevant? Is this person trying to manipulate me? The analytical mind activates, and with it, skepticism.

When you tell a story, something different happens. The brain shifts from evaluation to imagination. Instead of analyzing your claims, the client starts picturing the scenario. They see the characters. They feel the tension. They anticipate the outcome.

In that imaginative state, resistance drops. The client isn't being sold to. They're being transported. They're experiencing someone else's situation and drawing their own conclusions.

That's the secret. When you argue, you create opposition. When you story, you create identification. The client stops thinking "this salesperson wants something from me" and starts thinking "that could be me."

The best part? They reach the conclusion themselves. You didn't push them there. The story guided them, and they walked on their own. That kind of decision sticks.

...

The Three Questions

Every client has three questions running in their head. They'll never say them out loud, but the questions are always there, silently evaluating everything you say.

Has someone like me done this before?

What happened to them?

Will it work for me?

Data can't answer these questions. Charts can't answer them. Only stories can.

When you tell a story about a client who faced the same fear and made the leap, you answer question one. When you describe what happened, the outcome they achieved, you answer question two. When the client sees themselves in that story, they answer question three on their own.

A good story answers all three before the client realizes they were asking.

...

Buy Now, Refi Later

An agent on my team was working with buyers who wanted to wait for rates to drop before purchasing.

She could have pulled up charts. She could have explained the economics of timing the market. She could have made the mathematical case for why waiting was risky. All of that would have triggered resistance.

Instead, she told a story.

"Last year, I worked with a young couple in almost exactly your situation. They said the same thing: 'We'll wait for rates to fall.' Six months later, rates ticked down a quarter point. Just like they predicted. But in those six months, prices in their target neighborhood climbed twenty thousand dollars. They ended up paying more overall, even with the lower rate. And the home they'd originally loved? Sold to someone else."

She paused, then continued.

"Another client bought when rates were higher. Same timeframe. Found the home they wanted, locked it in, refinanced eight months later when rates dropped. They got the house and the rate. The difference? One family got the home they loved. The other paid more and lost time."

The buyers looked at each other. "We don't want to be the first couple."

They bought that week. No argument. No pressure. Just a story that let them see the consequences clearly.

• • •

The Overpriced Listing

Sellers want more than the market supports. One of the most common challenges in real estate. One of the hardest to win with logic alone.

An agent on my team faced exactly this. The seller wanted to list twenty-five thousand above what the comps supported. "My neighbor's house sold for more," they insisted.

She didn't argue. She told a story.

"Two months ago, I worked with a seller in a neighborhood similar to yours. They wanted to test the market with a higher price. I understood the impulse. Six weeks later, the home was still sitting. Traffic had dried up. The listing felt stale. When they finally reduced, buyers sensed weakness. Offers came in low. They sold for less than we could have achieved if we'd priced right from day one."

She let that settle, then offered the contrast.

"Another client, same market, priced strategically from the start. First week, multiple showings. Competitive tension built. Offers came in above asking. The difference? The first home chased the market down. The second made the market chase them."

Silence. Then the seller asked, "What price do you recommend?"

Listing went live at the strategic price. Multiple offers. Sold in days. No argument won that. The story did.

$$\bullet \ \bullet \ \bullet$$

The Anatomy of a Sales Story

Every effective sales story follows the same structure, whether you're conscious of it or not.

It starts with a character the client can identify with. Someone like them. Same fears, same situation, same hesitations. The more specific the details, the more real the character feels.

Then comes the struggle. The fear they faced. The objection they raised. The resistance that almost stopped them. This is where your client sees themselves. This is where identification happens.

Next is the shift. The moment of decision. What did the character choose? What pushed them from hesitation to action? This is the pivot point, the hinge the whole story turns on.

Then the outcome. What happened as a result? Success or failure, the consequence must be clear and concrete. Vague outcomes produce vague impact.

Finally, the implied lesson. You don't have to state it explicitly. Often more powerful if you don't. The client draws the conclusion themselves: "I can be the client who acted, or the one who waited. Which do I want to be?"

Character, struggle, shift, outcome, lesson. Master this structure, and you can turn any experience into a story that moves people.

• • •

The Story Bank

Titans don't wing it. They build a story bank.

Every deal adds another story. Every client interaction is raw material. Every objection overcome, every fear addressed, every success created becomes a story you can tell again.

Keep a running log. Write down what happened. Note the character, the struggle, the shift, the outcome. Capture details while they're fresh. A story remembered vaguely is a story told weakly.

Organize by objection. When a client says "I want to wait for rates to drop," you should know exactly which story to reach for. When they say "I think we should price higher," another story should be ready. When they say "I'm talking to other agents," you pull a different one.

Before important meetings, review your bank. Remind yourself which stories fit this client's situation. Walk in loaded with narratives that address exactly what they're likely to feel and fear.

Agents who stumble through objections haven't built their bank. Agents who handle everything smoothly have stories for every situation. Build yours, and you'll never be caught without the right words.

• • •

Micro-Stories

Not every story needs to be long. Sometimes two sentences hit harder than two minutes.

"A client waited for rates to drop. By the time they acted, prices had climbed. They paid more for less house."

Complete story. Character, decision, consequence. Twenty words. Five seconds to deliver. Lands like a punch.

Micro-stories work because they're unexpected. The client braces for a long pitch and gets a quick insight instead. The brevity makes it memorable. The speed makes it feel like wisdom, not salesmanship.

Build micro-stories for your most common objections. One or two sentences capturing an entire cautionary tale or success story. When time is short or attention thin, these are your weapons.

• • •

Story Plus Data

The most powerful combination? A story followed by the data that proves it.

Tell the story first. Let the client feel it, imagine it, identify with it. Then, while they're still in that emotional space, introduce the statistic that validates what they just experienced.

"That seller listed high and sat for weeks. When they finally reduced, they sold for less than we could have gotten originally. And here's the thing: that's not an outlier. Homes in this market that reduce after thirty days average ninety-two percent of list price. Homes priced right from day one? They average a hundred and one percent."

The story made it real. The data made it undeniable. Neither works as well alone. Together, almost impossible to argue with.

Lead with story, follow with data. Emotion opens the door. Logic locks it.

• • •

The Client as Hero

Here's where most agents get storytelling wrong: they make themselves the hero.

They tell stories about how they saved the deal. How their expertise rescued the client. How their brilliance turned disaster into triumph. Every story centers on how amazing the agent is.

The client doesn't care how amazing you are. They care about themselves. They want to see themselves in the story, not you.

In every story you tell, the client is the hero. They faced the fear. They made the brave decision. They achieved the outcome. You're just the guide who helped them get there.

Think of yourself as the trainer in a boxing movie, not the boxer. The mentor in a hero's journey, not the hero. Your client is Rocky. You're Mickey. Your client is Luke Skywalker. You're Yoda.

When you position the client as hero, they see themselves succeeding. When you position yourself as hero, they see you bragging. One builds trust. The other erodes it.

• • •

Stories are the oldest technology humans have for changing minds.

Before writing, before data, before PowerPoint, there were stories around fires. Tales that taught without lecturing. Narratives that shaped behavior without demanding compliance.

The clients you work with are no different from those ancient listeners. They resist being sold to. They resent being pressured. But they lean into a good story. They remember it. They retell it to their spouse that night. They make decisions based on it.

Build your story bank. Master the structure. Lead with narrative, follow with data. Make the client the hero. Practice until your stories feel like conversations, not performances.

Do this, and you stop sounding like a salesperson. You sound like a guide. A trusted advisor. Someone who's seen this before and knows how it ends.

Facts tell. Stories sell. Titans know the difference.

...

TITAN TRUTH

A good story never has to push.

PILLAR 4

RELATIONSHIPS

CHAPTER 10

Relationship Capital

How Titans of Sales Build Lifelong Clients

"One deal feeds you for a month. One relationship feeds you for life."

• • •

The commission check clears and everyone moves on.

The client starts unpacking boxes. The agent starts chasing the next deal. The transaction that consumed everyone's attention for weeks becomes a closed file, a line item, a memory that fades with each passing season.

This is how most agents operate. Close the deal, cash the check, hunt for the next one. An endless cycle of starting over. Every January resets to zero. Every month demands new leads because last month's clients are already forgotten.

Titans play a different game.

They understand that the closing table isn't the end. It's the beginning. The moment everyone else stops paying attention is precisely when Titans start building something that pays dividends for decades.

Relationship capital. The compound interest of sales.

• • •

The Math of Relationships

Every person you help knows 150 to 200 other people. That's the average sphere of influence. Friends, family, coworkers, neighbors, the people they see at church or the gym or their kid's soccer games.

When someone in that sphere asks, "Do you know a good agent?" your name either comes up or it doesn't. That moment, that question asked at a barbecue or in a break room or over dinner, determines business you'll never trace back to its source.

Now multiply. Ten clients become access to 2,000 people. Fifty clients become access to 10,000. A hundred clients, nurtured over years, become a network so vast that business finds you without effort.

But only if they remember you. Only if you've built enough relationship capital that your name surfaces when the question gets asked.

Agents who disappear after closing never access those 150 to 200 people. Agents who stay present, who nurture, who build capital over time, eventually stop chasing business entirely. Business chases them.

. . .

Layers of the Onion

Your CRM should be like layers of an onion.

At the center, your inner circle. Past clients who love you. Family and close friends. People who would refer you without hesitation, who defend you if someone speaks poorly of your work, who think of you first and only when real estate comes up.

Next layer out, your warm contacts. People you've met, built rapport with, stayed in touch with. They know you're in real estate. They'd probably use you if the situation arose. But the relationship needs nurturing to stay warm.

Further out, your broader network. Acquaintances. People who might recognize your name. They won't refer you unprompted, but if you stay present, if you keep adding value, they could move closer to center over time.

The goal isn't just adding names to outer layers. It's moving people inward. Taking a stranger and making them an acquaintance. Taking an acquaintance and making them a fan. Taking a fan and making them a lifelong advocate.

Every touch, every interaction, every moment of value either moves someone toward center or lets them drift toward the edge. Relationship capital is measured by how many people occupy your inner layers and how actively you're moving others inward.

...

The Connection Compass

For every person in your database, you should know their NEWS.

It's a system called the Connection Compass. Four directions that point you toward a real relationship. Four pieces of information that transform a name in your CRM into a person you actually know.

N — Next. Where are they headed? What are their goals? Are they thinking about moving, retiring, expanding their family, changing careers?

E — Energy. What lights them up? What do they do for fun? Sports, hobbies, travel, causes they care about.

W — Work. What do they do? Not just their job title, but what their work actually involves. Do they love it? Where do they see it going?

S — Soil. Their roots. Their foundation. Spouse, kids, parents. Where they grew up. The people and places that ground them.

When you know someone's NEWS, everything changes. Your follow-up becomes personal. Your conversations have depth. You can ask about the promotion they were chasing, the vacation they were planning, how their daughter's volleyball season went. They realize you actually listened. You actually remembered.

That's rare. Most salespeople don't remember. They're too busy thinking about the next pitch to retain what someone shared three months ago.

When you're the one who remembers, you stand apart. The Connection Compass transforms you from a salesperson in their contacts to a person who genuinely knows them. That transformation is worth more than any marketing campaign.

• • •

The Neighborhood Party

An agent on my team closed a deal in a neighborhood where she wanted to build presence. Instead of moving on to the next transaction, she did something different.

She threw a party.

Not for herself. For her clients. A housewarming party, but bigger. She invited the neighbors. Brought food. Made it easy for her clients to meet the people living around them, the people they'd wave to for years to come.

The clients were thrilled. They looked like the welcoming new neighbors, the kind of people you'd want on your street. The neighbors got free food and a chance to meet the new family. Everyone won.

And the agent? She met every homeowner on that block. She wasn't cold calling or door knocking. She was the person who threw the party. Associated with warmth, generosity, community.

Two of those neighbors listed with her within eighteen months. Neither transaction required a pitch. They already knew her. They already trusted her. The party deposited relationship capital into accounts she didn't know existed.

That's thinking beyond the transaction. That's building capital that compounds.

• • •

The Forgotten Client

An agent on my team met a homeowner at an open house. The homeowner mentioned they'd bought their current place years ago through a different agent.

"Are you going to use that agent when you sell?" my agent asked.

The homeowner shrugged. "I don't think so. We never heard from them again."

Never heard from them again. Years of potential relationship capital, evaporated. A client who would have been loyal, who would have referred, who would have returned, lost to silence.

That original agent probably thought they were busy. Probably thought they'd reach out eventually. Probably assumed the client would remember them when the time came. Wrong on every count.

The client didn't remember. The client felt forgotten. When someone feels forgotten, they don't feel loyalty. They feel nothing at all.

That homeowner listed with my agent. Not because my agent was better at selling homes. Because my agent was present when the other agent was absent. Presence beats talent when talent doesn't show up.

• • •

The Discipline of Staying Present

Relationship capital requires discipline. Not the heroic discipline of a single grand gesture, but the quiet discipline of consistent small touches over years.

A handwritten note on the anniversary of their purchase. A quick text when you see their neighborhood in the news. A holiday card that isn't about business, just gratitude. An invitation to a client event. A check-in call with no agenda other than genuine curiosity about how they're doing.

None of these touches close a deal. That's not the point. Each touch is a deposit into an account that pays out later, in ways you can't predict, at times you won't expect.

Agents who struggle with this want immediate returns. They send a note and expect a referral next week. When it doesn't come, they stop sending notes. They don't understand compound interest. They want day-trading returns from a long-term investment.

Titans play the long game. They make deposits without tracking immediate withdrawals. They trust the account is growing even when the balance isn't visible. Years later, when referrals flow and repeat business stacks and reputation precedes them, they understand what they built.

• • •

The Client Who Came Back

An agent on my team helped a young couple buy their first home. Starter home. Modest commission. The kind of deal some agents treat as a stepping stone to bigger things.

This agent didn't treat it that way. She treated it like the beginning of a relationship. Stayed in touch. Remembered their anniversary. Knew about their kids, their jobs, their plans.

Two years later, they called. Ready to upgrade. They'd outgrown the starter home faster than expected. She helped them sell the old place and buy the new one. Transactions two and three.

Five years after that, another call. The husband's parents needed to downsize. Could she help? She could. Sold the parents' home, helped them find something smaller. Transactions four and five.

Along the way, two referrals came from that original couple. Friends who asked who they'd used. The answer was easy. It was always the same answer. Transactions six and seven.

One starter home. Seven transactions. All because she understood that the first deal wasn't the end. It was the seed.

That's relationship capital compounding. Not one check, but a stream. Not one client, but a network. Not one transaction, but a career.

$$\bullet \bullet \bullet$$

Beyond Clients

Relationship capital isn't limited to clients.

Titans build capital with everyone. Colleagues, vendors, lenders, inspectors, contractors, title officers. Every person in the ecosystem of a transaction is a relationship worth nurturing.

The lender who trusts you sends referrals your way. The contractor who respects you recommends you to their clients. The title officer who knows you'll have clean files prioritizes your deals when things get busy.

Every handshake is a potential deposit. Every promise kept is interest earned. Every time you follow through when others don't, your account grows.

Over time, reputation becomes your moat. Deals find you because people trust you. Opportunities appear because people believe in you. Doors open that talent alone could never unlock.

Agents who treat vendors as disposable, who burn relationships for short-term gain, who think only clients matter, eventually find themselves isolated. Agents who build capital everywhere find themselves surrounded by people eager to help them succeed.

• • •

The commission check is not the goal. It's the byproduct.

The goal is relationship capital. An ever-growing account of trust, connection, and goodwill that produces returns long after any single transaction is forgotten.

Build your layers. Gather their NEWS. Stay present when others disappear. Make deposits without demanding immediate withdrawals. Think beyond clients to everyone in your orbit.

Do this for years, and something remarkable happens. The hustle softens. The desperation fades. Business arrives not because you chased it but because you earned it, relationship by relationship, deposit by deposit, trust by trust.

Commissions pay bills. Relationships build empires. Titans know which one to chase.

• • •

TITAN TRUTH

The closing table is the starting line.

CHAPTER 11

Trust Before Transaction

Earn the Right to Close

"People don't buy from the best salesperson. They buy from the one they trust."

• • •

The close isn't something you take. It's something you earn.

Most agents treat closing like a finish line they sprint toward. They learn the techniques. They memorize the scripts. They study pressure points and psychological triggers and ways to corner someone into saying yes. Then they wonder why clients resist, why deals fall apart, why victory feels hollow even when they win.

They've got it backwards.

The close isn't a technique you deploy at the end of a conversation. It's the natural conclusion of trust built from the beginning. When trust is present, the close happens almost by itself. When trust is absent, no technique in the world will save you.

Titans understand this. They don't chase transactions. They build trust. They know that if they get the trust right, the transaction follows. Every time.

Trust before transaction. That's the order. Reverse it, and you lose both.

• • •

Earning the Right

You don't have the right to ask for someone's business just because you showed up.

You haven't earned it by handing them a card. You haven't earned it by making a pitch. You haven't earned it by telling them how great you are or how many deals you've closed or how long you've been in the industry.

You earn the right to close by demonstrating value before you ask for anything. By solving a problem before you mention your services. By giving before you take.

This is the same principle that governs prospecting calls. You earn eight seconds, then two minutes, then twenty minutes, then the appointment. Each stage is earned by delivering value in the stage before.

The close works the same way. You earn the right to ask by proving you're worth trusting. You prove you're worth trusting by putting the client's interests ahead of your own, visibly and consistently, until they can't imagine working with anyone else.

When you've truly earned the right, you don't have to ask. They offer.

• • •

The Trust Account

Think of every relationship as a bank account. Every interaction is either a deposit or a withdrawal.

A deposit is anything that builds trust. Telling the truth when it's uncomfortable. Following through on a promise. Remembering something personal they mentioned. Giving advice that helps them even if it doesn't help you. Showing up when you said you would. Being the same person in every interaction, consistent and reliable.

A withdrawal is anything that erodes trust. A missed callback. A broken commitment. A moment where they sense you're more interested in the commission than in them. A time you oversold or overpromised. Any gap between what you said and what you did.

Most agents don't track their balance. They make withdrawals without realizing it. They show up to close and discover the account is overdrawn. The client resists, the agent blames the client. But the agent emptied the account themselves.

Titans obsess over deposits. They build a surplus so large that when they finally ask for the business, the answer is automatic. The client doesn't hesitate because the trust account is overflowing. The yes was already there, waiting to be released.

Make deposits. Avoid withdrawals. Check your balance before you try to close.

• • •

The Client Who Wasn't Ready

An agent on my team met with a couple who wanted to buy a home. Excited. Eager. Ready to start looking immediately.

Except they weren't ready. Their finances told a different story. Credit issues. Debt that needed attention. A down payment that wasn't quite there.

Most agents would have found a way. Stretched them into something they could technically afford. Engineered a deal that got the commission now and left the consequences for later. The couple was willing. The transaction was possible.

This agent did something different. She told them the truth.

"Wait six months. Pay down this debt. Build your credit score. Save a little more. When you're ready, I'll be here."

They were stunned. No one had ever told them to wait. They expected a pitch, not patience. Pressure, not protection.

Six months later, they called. Bought a home they could actually afford, with terms that didn't stretch them thin. Referred two friends within the year. That single act of putting trust before transaction turned into three deals and a relationship that still produces referrals today.

The commission she didn't take in January became three commissions by December. That's the math of trust.

• • •

Radical Honesty

Most salespeople hide their weaknesses. They dodge uncomfortable questions. They spin negatives into positives. They hope the client doesn't notice the gap between pitch and reality.

Titans do the opposite. They put weaknesses on the table before the client discovers them.

If a competitor charges lower fees, they acknowledge it. If their service has a limitation, they disclose it. If a home has a flaw, they point it out before the inspection does. If they're not the right fit for what the client needs, they say so.

This feels counterintuitive. Why highlight your own weaknesses? Why give the client a reason to hesitate?

Because the moment you prove you'll tell the truth even when it costs you, something shifts. The client stops wondering what you're hiding. They stop questioning your motives. They start trusting you in a way they don't trust anyone who only shows them the highlight reel.

Radical honesty is a massive deposit into the trust account. It signals you're playing a different game. That signal is worth more than whatever short-term advantage you gave up by being transparent.

• • •

The Desperation Signal

Clients can smell desperation. They sense when you need the deal more than you want to help them. They feel the pressure beneath your words, even when your words are polished and professional.

Desperation is a withdrawal from the trust account. Every time. It signals that your interests come first. It tells the client you're not focused on them, you're focused on the close. The moment they sense that, resistance rises.

The irony is brutal. The harder you chase the transaction, the more it runs away. Push too hard and the client retreats. Apply pressure and they find reasons to hesitate. Force the close and even if you get the signature, you lose the relationship.

Titans approach from abundance, not scarcity. They don't need any single deal because they've built a pipeline of relationships. They can afford to be patient because they're not desperate. That calm confidence draws clients in instead of pushing them away.

Remove the desperation and trust grows. Let trust grow and the deals become inevitable.

• • •

The Slow Play

Sometimes the fastest path to a closed deal is to slow down.

An agent on my team was working with a buyer who seemed ready to move. They'd seen houses. They'd found one they liked. The logical next step was to write an offer.

But something felt off. The buyer kept asking questions already answered. They wanted to see the house again. They hesitated when discussing next steps.

Instead of pushing toward the offer, the agent slowed down. "It seems like something's on your mind. What's making you hesitate?"

The buyer exhaled. There was a concern they hadn't voiced. A fear about the neighborhood. A worry about overextending. Things they'd been holding back because they didn't want to seem difficult.

The agent addressed each concern. Some were resolved with information. One required looking at a different property. The process took another two weeks.

When they finally closed, it was on the right house with complete confidence. No buyer's remorse. No second-guessing. The buyer referred three families over the next two years.

The agent who pushed would have gotten a faster close and a weaker relationship. The agent who slowed down got a client for life.

• • •

Trust Compounds

A transaction is a one-time event. Trust is a compounding asset.

When you earn someone's trust, you don't just earn their business today. You earn their business next time. You earn introductions to their friends. You earn their defense when someone speaks poorly of you. You earn a relationship that produces value long after the original transaction is forgotten.

This is the math most agents miss. They optimize for the immediate close and sacrifice the compound returns. They take the withdrawal today without building the balance that would pay dividends for decades.

Titans think in years, not transactions. They know one client fully trusted becomes multiple clients over time. They know the reputation built by putting trust first attracts more business than any marketing campaign.

The transaction feeds you once. Trust feeds you forever.

• • •

You can close without trust. It happens every day. High-pressure tactics work on some people some of the time. You can push someone across the line if you're skilled enough and they're uncertain enough.

But those deals don't come back. Those clients don't refer. Those relationships end at the closing table.

Titans build something different. They build trust first, and the close becomes a natural conclusion rather than a battle. They earn the right before they exercise it. They make deposits before withdrawals. They slow down when others speed up.

The result is a career where clients seek you out. Where referrals arrive without asking. Where the close feels less like a technique and more like a handshake between people who trust each other.

Trust before transaction. Always. The deals will follow.

• • •

TITAN TRUTH

Trust closes quietly.

CHAPTER 12

Legendary Moments

The Details That Make You Unforgettable

"People don't remember average. They remember moments."

• • •

Every client leaves with a story.

The only question is whether it's worth telling.

Most transactions produce forgettable stories. "They were fine. Got the job done. Professional enough." The kind of story that dies in the telling. No one leans in. No one asks for details. No one remembers the agent's name six months later.

Then there are the other stories. The ones clients can't wait to share. "You won't believe what our agent did." The stories that get told at dinner parties, repeated at work, shared with anyone who mentions real estate. The stories that generate referrals for years without a single ask.

The difference between forgettable and legendary isn't skill. It isn't market knowledge. It isn't years of experience. It's the moment. The one gesture, one detail, one act of unexpected care that transforms a transaction into a story worth telling.

Titans don't leave these moments to chance. They create them.

• • •

The Peak-End Rule

Psychologists discovered something fascinating about how humans remember experiences. We don't judge an experience by its total length or by averaging every moment together. We judge it by two things: the most intense moment and how it ended.

They call it the Peak-End Rule.

Think about a vacation. Ten days somewhere, but what you remember is one magical afternoon and the final evening. A great movie ruined by a weak ending. A mediocre meal made memorable by extraordinary dessert.

Sales works the same way. Your client won't replay every interaction. They'll remember the peak, the moment of highest emotional intensity, and they'll remember the end, how the experience concluded.

This means two things. First, create peaks on purpose. Moments of genuine surprise, care, or impact that rise above routine. Second, end strong. The final impression matters as much as the first.

Titans engineer both. They don't hope for legendary moments. They design them.

• • •

The Champagne in the Trunk

An agent on my team didn't have the biggest marketing budget. No billboards. No massive ad spend. What he had was intention and creativity.

He started keeping a bottle of champagne and two glasses in his trunk. Standard enough. Plenty of agents do closing gifts. But here's the detail that made it legendary: each bottle had a handwritten note taped to it.

"This house will hold your laughter, your fights, your kids' first steps. Tonight, toast to the first page of that story."

One couple arrived at their empty new home exhausted from moving boxes. He opened the trunk, handed them the champagne with the note, and snapped a candid photo of them clinking glasses in the bare living room. Nothing staged. Just two tired, happy people beginning something new.

Months later, when he stopped by for a check-in, that photo was framed on their mantle.

He didn't just close a deal. He created a memory. The champagne cost twelve dollars. The moment was priceless.

• • •

The Neighborhood Dinner

I helped a family purchase a home in a neighborhood where I'd sold a house two years earlier. As the new transaction wrapped up and the closing date approached, I had an idea.

I invited both families to dinner.

Not a client appreciation event with fifty people and name tags. A real dinner. One table. Two families who were about to become neighbors but had never met.

The evening started with the usual small talk. Where are you from? What do you do? How old are your kids? But somewhere between appetizers and dessert, something shifted. The families discovered their children were close in age. They'd gone through similar struggles buying their first homes. They shared the same nervous excitement about the neighborhood, the same hopes for what this next chapter might hold.

By the end of the night, they weren't just neighbors. They were friends.

I paid for that first dinner. Not because it was required. Not because I expected anything in return. Because I wanted to give these families something more valuable than a closing gift. I wanted to give them community.

That was years ago. The dinner became a tradition. Every year, the three households meet,the two families and me. We catch up on kids' milestones, career changes, life's turns. I don't pay anymore. Everyone covers their own now. It stopped being a client dinner a long time ago. It's just dinner with friends.

Those two families have referred more business than any marketing campaign ever could. But that's not why I keep showing up. I keep showing up because legendary moments aren't just about creating memories for clients. Sometimes they're about creating something you want to be part of too.

• • •

The Framed Blueprint

A family built their dream home from the ground up. Years of sacrifice. Overtime shifts. Prayers answered. To them, it wasn't lumber and drywall. It was everything they'd worked toward.

At the final walkthrough, their agent surprised them with something unexpected.

She had taken the original blueprint, still smudged with pencil lines and stained with coffee rings, and asked every contractor who touched the house to sign it. But the signatures weren't just names. They were messages.

The framer wrote, "May your kids always feel safe here." The carpenter who built the staircase wrote, "I built this for your family to climb." The one who installed the kitchen island wrote, "This is where you'll make memories."

When the family saw it, they cried. It wasn't paper. It was the fingerprints of everyone who built their dream.

That blueprint still hangs framed in their living room. The agent who thought to create that moment? She's handled three generations of that family's real estate. Not because she's the best negotiator in town. Because she understood that details are the difference.

• • •

The Veteran's Keys

A veteran was buying his first home. An agent on my team handled the transaction and learned something important during the process: this purchase meant more than shelter. It was proof of a life rebuilt after service, sacrifice, and struggle.

On closing day, the agent arranged for the keys to be delivered in a small wooden box. Inside, folded neatly beneath the keys, was an American flag. A fellow veteran, still in uniform, handed over the box and saluted.

The buyer's hands trembled as he opened it. For a full minute, he said nothing. Just hugged the box to his chest, tears streaming down his face. Finally, he whispered, "This means more than the house."

That story spread through his entire unit. The agent became the go-to for veteran referrals in the community. Not because of an ad. Not because of a mailer. Because he created a moment that honored something sacred.

The wooden box and flag cost maybe fifty dollars. The value of what it represented? Immeasurable.

• • •

The Quiet Moments

Not every legendary moment requires a grand gesture. Some are quiet. Ordinary, even. But no less powerful.

An agent on my team remembered after a single showing that her client liked vanilla lattes with two pumps, not three. Every appointment after that, she brought one. The client later joked, "She knew my coffee order better than my husband did." That kind of attention cements loyalty.

Another agent skipped the fancy closing gift basket. Instead, on moving day, he had the family's favorite local pizza delivered with a handwritten note: "Welcome home. First meal is on me. Just don't eat it on the carpet." They still laugh about it years later.

Another stayed on the phone while a panicked client cried about financing that might fall through. At the end, he said, "Sleep tonight. I'll carry the worry until morning." That single sentence transformed the relationship.

Small doesn't mean insignificant. Sometimes the smallest moments make the biggest impressions.

• • •

Seeing the Person

Legendary moments work because they're not about you. They're about the client.

They prove you see them. Not as a transaction. Not as a commission check. As a person with a story, a dream, and a future. Someone worth paying attention to.

That's why generic gifts fall flat. A fruit basket says, "I do this for everyone." A gift that connects to something personal they mentioned says, "I was listening. I remembered. You matter."

The difference between forgettable and legendary is personalization. The proof that you noticed the details that make them who they are.

This requires paying attention. Keeping notes. Gathering their NEWS, the details that matter. The legendary moment doesn't come from a playbook. It comes from knowing the person well enough to create something that could only be for them.

• • •

The Cost of Forgettable

What happens if you skip the legendary moments? Nothing dramatic. The deal still closes. The client still says thank you. They might even leave a positive review.

But they won't remember you.

Six months later, when their coworker mentions they're thinking about buying, your name won't surface. Two years later, when they're ready to sell, they'll search their email to remember who helped them buy. You'll be a vague recollection, not a vivid story.

Forgettable agents deliver transactions. They do the job competently. Check the boxes. And they spend the rest of their careers chasing new business because their past clients don't remember them well enough to refer.

Titans deliver transformations. They create moments that become stories. Those stories spread without effort, generating referrals for years after the transaction closes.

• • •

Anyone can close a deal.

The paperwork gets signed. The keys get handed over. The transaction completes. This is the minimum. This is what average agents do.

Titans do something more. They look for the moment that will matter. They think about what would surprise this particular client, what would make them feel seen, what would turn a transaction into a story worth telling.

It doesn't require a big budget. Champagne costs twelve dollars. A handwritten note costs nothing. Pizza delivery is thirty bucks. A dinner for two families, less than you'd spend on a closing gift. The investment is minimal. The return is a client who remembers you forever.

Create the peak. End strong. Make them feel like the only client you've ever had.

The details are the difference. The moments are the legacy.

• • •

TITAN TRUTH

Be the story they tell.

NEGOTIATION

CHAPTER 13

10% Opinion, 90% Delivery

What Top Closers Know

"Deals don't collapse because of numbers. They collapse because of negotiators."

• • •

It was supposed to be a routine deal.

The buyers loved the house. The sellers were ready to move. We were under contract, everything smooth. Then the inspection report landed.

Suddenly, excitement turned to tension. The buyers wanted fifteen thousand off for repairs. The sellers were insulted. They swore half the items were cosmetic and the rest exaggerated. Both sides stared at me like I was the referee in a heavyweight fight.

Every instinct told me to jump in. Explain. Justify. Mediate. But I didn't.

I stayed silent.

The sellers filled the gap first. "We're not giving fifteen thousand. Maybe seventy-five hundred."

The buyers glanced at me, expecting a response. I nodded calmly. Still silent.

Then the buyers blinked. "If they'll cover ten thousand, we'll move forward."

In less than three minutes, fifteen thousand became ten thousand. Not because I argued better. Because negotiation isn't about who talks more. It's about who frames the game, who controls the pace, and who knows when silence speaks louder than words.

Titans don't fight harder. They negotiate smarter.

• • •

Psychology First

Negotiation isn't numbers first. It's psychology first.

There's a truth I come back to constantly: ten percent of conflict is due to difference in opinion, and ninety percent is due to delivery and tone of voice. Read that again. Ninety percent. The words matter far less than how you say them.

People under pressure reveal who they are. Some panic. Some bluff. Some overcompensate with aggression. The way you show up in that moment determines everything that follows.

Psychologists call it mirroring affective states. If you're nervous, your clients and counterparts feel it. If you're composed, they borrow your composure. Calm is contagious. So is panic.

The best negotiators don't just prepare their numbers. They prepare their state. They walk into the room centered, neutral, ready. Not because they don't feel pressure. Because they've learned not to transmit it.

When everyone else is reacting, Titans are choosing. That's the edge.

• • •

The Power of Silence

Silence isn't passive. It's a weapon.

Most salespeople rush to fill the void. They discount too soon. They justify too much. They talk until their leverage evaporates. Every unnecessary word is a concession they didn't have to make.

Titans use silence to force the other side to reveal more than they intended. In an inspection negotiation, silence might get the seller to offer a concession before you even counter. In a multiple-offer scenario, silence might make the listing agent reveal another buyer's weakness.

Silence communicates something words can't: I'm not desperate. I'm not rushing. I'm in control.

The person who speaks first after a tense moment usually loses. Let them speak first.

• • •

Framing Over Fighting

Amateurs argue. Titans frame.

When a seller wants to overprice, the amateur argues why they're wrong. The Titan shows a market analysis beside homes that sat stale for months, then asks: "Do you want to win the neighborhood beauty contest, or win the closing table?"

When a buyer thinks a price is too high, the amateur says "This is too high." The Titan says: "Here's how this price compares to the three most recent closings. If we go higher, you're paying tomorrow's price today. Is that a risk you're willing to take?"

Notice the difference. The amateur fights the person. The Titan frames the choice. One creates resistance. The other creates clarity.

You don't win negotiations by proving you're right. You win by helping people see their options clearly enough to choose the path you've already mapped.

Frame the choices. Let them decide. Guide, don't push.

• • •

The Inspection Graveyard

The inspection phase is where deals go to die.

Buyers see a forty-page report and suddenly think the house is a lemon. Sellers see the same report and believe the buyers are nitpicking. Both sides dig in. Emotions run hot. What should be a negotiation becomes a war.

Here's what Titans know: every inspection is a negotiation test. Not a test of who's right about the furnace or the roof or the outlet that doesn't work. A test of who can keep the deal alive.

One phrase I use constantly during inspections: "Let's focus on what it takes to keep this deal alive, not what it takes to win an argument."

That resets the table. The goal isn't proving a point. It's getting to closing. Arguments feel good in the moment and kill deals in the long run.

When tensions rise during inspections, ask yourself: Am I fighting to win the argument or fighting to save the deal? Only one matters.

• • •

The Appraisal Gap

An agent on my team faced a nightmare scenario. The appraisal came in twenty thousand short of contract price. Buyers panicked. Sellers raged. The deal looked dead.

Instead of fighting the number, she reframed.

"We have three levers," she told both sides. "The buyer brings cash to cover the gap. The seller lowers the price. Or we meet in the middle. Those are the paths. Which one gets us to closing?"

Everyone calmed down. Options clear. Both sides conceded ten thousand. Deal saved.

The magic wasn't in the math. It was in controlling the frame. Instead of a twenty-thousand-dollar problem, it became a choice between three paths. Instead of an argument about who was right, it became collaboration toward a shared goal.

When deals hit obstacles, don't debate the obstacle. Present the paths around it.

• • •

The Ego Trap

Most deals don't die because of price. They die because of pride.

Sellers feel insulted by a low offer. Buyers feel taken advantage of by a counter. Someone's ego gets bruised, and suddenly the negotiation isn't about the house anymore. It's about winning. About not being the one who blinked.

Titans know how to defuse ego. They depersonalize the fight.

"This isn't about you versus them. It's about what the market will support."

"The numbers aren't personal. They're just numbers."

"We're not fighting each other. We're solving a puzzle together."

By shifting from personal to professional, from combat to collaboration, Titans protect deals from emotional collapse. They give people permission to back down without losing face.

Protect egos. Save deals. The pride isn't worth the dream home your client loses.

• • •

The Rookie and the Veteran

I once coached two agents through similar inspection negotiations. Same situation. Completely different outcomes.

The rookie panicked. She fought every line item. Argued with the inspector's language. Took every request personally. Defended her clients like she was in a courtroom instead of a negotiation. The deal fell apart.

The veteran stayed calm. He reframed each request in terms of cost versus value. "Replacing that outlet costs a hundred fifty dollars. Are we really going to lose a four-hundred-thousand-dollar deal over a hundred fifty dollars?" He kept perspective when everyone else lost theirs. The deal closed.

Same facts. Different frames. One agent saw a battle to win. The other saw a problem to solve.

Negotiation is rarely about facts. It's about framing and emotional control. Master those, and the facts take care of themselves.

• • •

The Walk-Away Line

Every Titan has a line they won't cross.

They don't cling to bad deals. They don't beg. They don't sacrifice their clients' interests to salvage a commission. They know when to fight and when to walk.

Here's the paradox: the more willing you are to walk away, the less often you'll have to. Walking away is power. The other side can feel it. When they sense you're not desperate, when they realize you'll actually leave the table, they negotiate differently.

Desperation invites exploitation. Willingness to walk commands respect.

Know your line before you enter the room. Communicate it clearly. Honor it. That clarity protects you from deals you should never have made.

• • •

Reputation as Leverage

In sales, your reputation becomes your leverage.

If agents in your market know you fight dirty, they avoid you. They warn their clients. They approach every negotiation defensively, ready for tricks. You spend energy overcoming resistance you created yourself.

If agents know you're calm, fair, and sharp, they want to work with you. They trust the process. They enter negotiations expecting a reasonable outcome, which makes reasonable outcomes more likely.

Your reputation saves your clients money before you even speak. It opens doors that stay locked for others. It creates goodwill that smooths negotiations you haven't started yet.

Titans negotiate not just for this deal, but for the hundred deals their name will touch. Every negotiation builds or erodes the reputation that makes the next one easier or harder.

• • •

Titans don't win negotiations by shouting louder or arguing longer.

They win by staying calm when others panic. By framing choices when others fight. By knowing when silence speaks louder than words. By protecting egos while protecting deals. By being willing to walk away and rarely having to.

The best negotiators don't feel like negotiators at all. They feel like guides. Problem-solvers. The person everyone wants in the room when stakes are high because they make hard conversations feel manageable.

Prepare your state, not just your numbers. Frame don't fight. Use silence as a tool. Know your walk-away line. Build a reputation that negotiates for you before you open your mouth.

Deals don't collapse because of numbers. They collapse because of negotiators. Be the one who saves them.

• • •

TITAN TRUTH

Calm is contagious. So is panic.

CHAPTER 14

Breaking the Barrier

Closing What Others Can't

"Every deal has one barrier. Find it. Remove it. Close."

• • •

The agent called me in a panic.

His buyers had searched eight months. Written four offers. Lost every one. Now they'd found the house, perfect neighborhood, right price, everything aligned. Two competing offers coming. Deadline: five o'clock.

"They won't pull the trigger," he said. "I've explained everything. Shown them the comps. They just keep saying they need to think about it."

I asked one question: "What are they actually afraid of?"

Silence.

"I don't know. They just keep stalling."

I told him to call them back. Forget the house. Forget the deadline. Ask one thing: "What's making you hesitate right now?"

Twenty minutes later, he had the answer. The wife's father had lost his job two months ago. They weren't worried about the house. They were worried about helping her parents. That fear had been poisoning every decision, never spoken, sitting beneath every conversation like a stone.

Once they said it out loud, everything shifted. They talked it through. Ran the numbers. Realized they could handle both scenarios. By four-thirty, the offer was in. By eight, accepted.

The house didn't change. The market didn't change. The deadline didn't change. What changed: the real barrier got named. And the moment it was named, it could be removed.

• • •

The Invisible Barrier

Here's what most agents never learn: the reason a deal stalls is almost never the reason they give you.

Buyer says price is too high. Price isn't the problem. Seller says they're not ready. Timing isn't the issue. Client says they need to think. Thinking isn't what they need.

Behind every surface objection lives an invisible barrier. A fear they haven't articulated. A concern they're embarrassed to voice. A person not in the room who controls the outcome. A wound from the past bleeding into the present.

Average agents fight surface objections. They argue price. Push timing. Pile on data, logic, pressure. The deal dies anyway. Not because they weren't persuasive. Because they were solving the wrong problem.

Titans don't fight surfaces. They find the barrier beneath.

• • •

The Five Hidden Barriers

Thousands of deals have taught me this: almost every stalled transaction traces back to one of five hidden barriers. Master them, and you'll close deals other agents abandon.

Barrier One: The Ghost at the Table

Someone not present is controlling the decision.

The father-in-law who thinks they're overpaying. The friend convinced the market's crashing. The adult child who hasn't weighed in. The business partner who approves anything over a certain amount. The ex-spouse whose opinion still carries weight.

Your client won't mention the ghost. Admitting they're not the real decision-maker feels like weakness. So they stall. Hedge. Find reasons to delay. You're negotiating with the person in front of you. The ghost makes the actual call.

Telltale sign: sudden hesitation after apparent agreement. "I just need to run it by..." and "Let me talk to..." are ghost alerts. Until you identify the ghost and bring them into the conversation, even indirectly, the deal stays frozen.

Barrier Two: The Past Wound

A bad experience is making them gun-shy.

Burned on an inspection ten years ago. Parents lost a house in the crash. Trusted an agent who ghosted them after closing. Made an offer once, got emotionally invested, lost to a higher bidder. Renovated a property that became a nightmare.

Past wounds create present paralysis. Your client isn't evaluating this deal on its merits. They're protecting themselves from a pain they swore they'd never feel again. The wound might be theirs. Or inherited from someone they trust.

Telltale sign: disproportionate caution. Excessive questions about unlikely scenarios. References to something that "happened before" or "happened to someone I know." Resistance that doesn't match the actual risk.

Barrier Three: The Unspoken Fear

A concern they're too embarrassed to voice.

Worried they can't actually afford it. Scared they'll hate the neighborhood. Don't understand the mortgage terms and don't want to look stupid asking. Think something's wrong that nobody's telling them. Terrified of buyer's remorse.

Unspoken fears fester in silence. The longer they go unnamed, the more power they gain. Your client won't volunteer it, admitting fear feels like weakness. So they hide behind logic. More time needed. More research required. Price concerns that aren't about price.

Telltale sign: vague resistance without clear reasoning. "Something just doesn't feel right", but they can't articulate what. Analysis paralysis. One more house to see, one more report to review, one more night to sleep on it.

Barrier Four: The Timing Trap

An external factor has them frozen.

Waiting on a job transfer. A bonus that might come through. An inheritance in probate. A lease that doesn't end for three months. A child's school year. A health issue. A wedding, a divorce, a retirement on the horizon.

The timing trap creates deals that look ready but won't move. Your client wants to buy. They're motivated. Found the right house. But something external has them handcuffed, and they won't explain what.

Telltale sign: interest without urgency. Engagement without commitment. They love the house but can't write the offer today. Want to move "soon" but can't define when.

Barrier Five: The Trust Gap

They haven't fully committed to you, the process, or the market.

Wondering if another agent might be better. Not convinced the market won't drop next month. Suspect the inspection process has blind spots. Read articles about hidden fees and predatory practices. Don't believe anyone in real estate has their best interest at heart.

The trust gap makes every recommendation suspect. Your client questions your judgment, not because you've done anything wrong, but because they haven't bought in. Until trust is established, no logic or urgency moves them.

Telltale sign: second-guessing. Wanting other opinions. Researching behind your back. Questions that feel like tests. Agreeing in the meeting, not following through after.

• • •

The Diagnostic Questions

Finding the barrier requires asking the right questions the right way. Not interrogating, exploring. Not pressuring, inviting.

When a deal stalls, work through these in your mind first. Then ask the ones that fit.

To find the Ghost:

"Who else will be affected by this decision?" "Is there anyone whose input you're waiting on?" "If you had to explain this to someone important, what would their concerns be?"

To find the Past Wound:

"Have you been through this before? How did it go?" "What's the worst-case scenario you're worried about?" "Is anything from a past experience making you cautious?"

To find the Unspoken Fear:

"Completely honest, what's the one thing making you hesitate?" "What would need to be true for you to feel totally confident?" "Is there something we haven't talked about?"

To find the Timing Trap:

"Is something happening soon that affects this?" "If everything was perfect, could you move forward today?" "What would need to happen for the timing to feel right?"

To find the Trust Gap:

"What questions haven't we covered?" "Is anything about this process unclear?" "Scale of one to ten, how confident do you feel, and what would make it a ten?"

Don't ask every question. Listen for which barrier is present. Probe deeper. The barrier reveals itself not in the first answer, but in the third.

• • •

The Removal Protocol

Each barrier requires a different removal approach.

Removing the Ghost:

Bring them into the conversation. "Should we schedule a call so I can walk them through the numbers?" "Can I address their concerns directly?" Don't fight the ghost for control. Include them. Answer their objections even when they're not in the room. Arm your client to advocate.

Removing the Past Wound:

Acknowledge it. Validate it. Then separate it from the present. "That sounds awful. I understand the caution. Here's what's different this time..." Show specifically how this situation isn't that situation. The wound must be honored before it can be released.

Removing the Unspoken Fear:

Create permission to say the unsayable. "I've had clients worried about that. Is it on your mind?" When they voice it, don't dismiss it. Explore it. Fear loses half its power the moment it's spoken. The other half dissolves when addressed directly.

Removing the Timing Trap:

Either solve for the timing or show why waiting costs more than moving. "If the transfer doesn't happen, what then?" "Let's look at what three months actually costs in this market." Sometimes timing is real and the deal should wait. But often timing is a shield for another barrier underneath.

Removing the Trust Gap:

You can't argue someone into trust. Demonstrate it. Over-communicate. Follow through on small things. Offer references. Be transparent about your incentives. Give information that goes against your interest. Trust gaps close through consistency, not persuasion.

• • •

The Resurrection

There's a special category of deals other agents have abandoned. Clients who went cold. Transactions that fell apart. "Dead" files collecting dust.

Titans know most of those deals aren't dead. They're undiagnosed.

An agent on my team inherited a lead four previous agents had given up on. The client had been looking for two years. Every agent had the same experience: enthusiastic showings, promising conversations, then sudden silence. Ghosted.

Instead of showing more houses, my agent asked: "What made you stop working with the last four agents?"

The client paused. Then admitted what she'd never told anyone: her husband had been diagnosed with a chronic illness two years ago. They wanted to buy, but she was terrified of a thirty-year mortgage when she didn't know what the next five years would bring. Every time she got close to an offer, fear overwhelmed her.

Once named, the barrier could be addressed. They talked contingencies. Ran scenarios. Calculated what staying in their rental actually cost versus buying now. Discussed what her husband wanted.

Six weeks later, they closed. Not because my agent showed a better house. Because she found the barrier four agents missed.

Every "dead" lead is a barrier waiting to be found. The clients who ghosted you, the deals that collapsed, the transactions that died for reasons you never understood, they're not gone. They're hiding behind a barrier no one took time to find.

• • •

The Titan's Edge

This is the skill that separates closers from everyone else.

Average agents see a stalled deal and push harder. Argue more. Follow up relentlessly. Wonder why logic fails and motivation fades. They lose deals they should have won and never understand why.

Titans see a stalled deal and ask: What's the barrier I haven't found?

Behind every "no" is a story. Behind every stall is a fear. Behind every dead deal is an undiagnosed barrier. Titans don't accept surface objections. They dig until they find what's really blocking the path.

When they find it, they remove it. Not through pressure. Not through persuasion. Through understanding.

See deals as puzzles to solve, not battles to win. Your closing rate transforms. You stop losing to invisible obstacles. You start winning deals others can't.

• • •

Every deal has one barrier.

It hides behind logic that doesn't add up. Resistance that seems irrational. A client who wants to move forward but can't. A ghost not in the room. A wound that hasn't healed. A fear never spoken. Timing that isn't right. Trust that hasn't been earned.

Your job isn't to argue louder. It's to see deeper.

Find the barrier others miss. Name what hasn't been named. Address what everyone ignores. That's how you close what others can't. Resurrect what others abandoned. Become the person clients call when everything seems impossible.

Stop fighting surfaces.

Find it. Remove it. Close.

• • •

TITAN TRUTH

The barrier is never what they say it is.

CHAPTER 15

Nobody Buys a House

Sell the Outcome

"Nobody buys a house. They buy a life."

• • •

Stop talking about what you do.

Most agents walk into every conversation armed with features. I'll list your home on the MLS. I'll do professional photography. I'll hold open houses. I'll negotiate on your behalf. I have twenty years of experience. I've closed hundreds of deals.

The client nods politely. Eyes glaze over. They've heard this from every agent they've talked to. It all sounds the same.

Because it is the same. Features are commodities. Every agent has them. Listing features gets you compared. And when you're compared on features, you're compared on price.

Titans don't sell features. They sell outcomes.

They don't talk about what they do. They talk about what the client gets. Not the process. The result. Not the service. The transformation.

The value conversation isn't about proving you're worth your fee. It's about painting a picture so vivid that the fee becomes irrelevant.

• • •

The Shift

Features describe what you do. Outcomes describe what they get.

"I'll market your home aggressively" is a feature. "Your home sells faster so you can move into your new place before school starts" is an outcome.

"I have access to off-market listings" is a feature. "You'll see homes your competition doesn't even know exist" is an outcome.

"I'll handle all the negotiations" is a feature. "You won't leave money on the table or agree to terms that hurt you" is an outcome.

The shift is subtle but the impact is massive. Features make clients think, "So what?" Outcomes make them think, "That's exactly what I need."

Every feature you mention should connect to an outcome they care about. If it doesn't, don't mention it. No one cares what you do. Everyone cares what they get.

Make the shift. Watch the conversation change.

• • •

The Movie Set

A staged home is a movie set.

Nobody lives like that. The table is set with wine glasses and cloth napkins for a dinner party that's never happening. Fresh fruit in a bowl that will never be eaten. The bed has fourteen pillows arranged in a way no human would sleep on. Fancy soap sits untouched by the sink.

Completely artificial. And it works.

Because buyers aren't buying the house. They're buying the life they imagine living in it. The staged home doesn't show them square footage and closet space. It shows them dinner parties with friends. Lazy Sunday mornings. The life they want to step into.

Staging sells the outcome, not the product. The feeling, not the features. That's why a few hundred dollars in staging can add thousands to a sale price. The buyer isn't paying for the property. They're paying for the vision of who they become when they live there.

That's selling the outcome. You're not showing them what the house is. You're showing them what their life could be.

• • •

The Gazebo

A seller once walked me through her backyard and stopped at a weathered gazebo. Nothing special. Needed paint. The wood was showing its age.

But she looked at it and her eyes filled with tears. "My kids got married under that gazebo."

She wasn't selling a structure. She was selling thirty years of memories. Summer barbecues. Birthday parties. Her daughter's wedding reception. The place where her family became a family.

Sellers don't see square footage. They see their lives. Every room holds a memory. Every scratch on the floor tells a story. When they price their home, they're not pricing a building. They're pricing what it meant to them.

Understanding this changes the value conversation. You're not just discussing market comps and pricing strategy. You're honoring what the home represents while helping them see what the market will actually pay.

The gazebo reminds us that real estate is never just real estate. For buyers, it's the life they're stepping into. For sellers, it's the life they're leaving behind. Titans understand both.

• • •

The Wealth Conversation

Most buyers think they're buying a monthly payment. They compare mortgage rates. They calculate what they can afford. They see a house as an expense.

Titans reframe the conversation. You're not buying a payment. You're buying equity that grows while you sleep.

That equity becomes your daughter's college tuition. It becomes the down payment on your son's first home. It becomes a HELOC that lets you start a business or renovate the kitchen or take the trip you've been postponing for years. It becomes retirement security. Generational wealth. A legacy.

When a first-time buyer hesitates at the price, they're thinking about the payment. When you paint the picture of what that equity becomes over ten, twenty, thirty years, they start thinking about the outcome.

The house is the vehicle. The wealth is the destination. Sell the destination.

This isn't manipulation. It's truth. Homeownership is one of the most powerful wealth-building tools that exists. Most people just don't think about it that way until someone shows them.

• • •

Your Value, Their Outcome

When a client questions your fee, the amateur gets defensive. They justify. They explain all the work they do. They list credentials. They argue.

The Titan redirects to outcomes.

"What's it worth to you to sell in three weeks instead of three months?" "What's it worth to avoid the mistake that costs you twenty thousand dollars because you didn't know the inspection red flags?" "What's it worth to have someone who's done this five hundred times guiding you through the biggest financial decision of your life?"

You're not defending what you charge. You're illuminating what they receive. The fee becomes context for the value, not a number to negotiate down.

There are probably a hundred agents they could hire. Most will list the same features. The agent who wins connects those features to outcomes that matter to this specific client.

Stop justifying your fee. Start painting what they get for it.

. . .

Work in Ranges

Never give an exact price. Work in ranges.

When a seller asks what their home is worth, the amateur blurts out a number. "I think we can get four twenty-five." Now that number is an anchor. Everything gets compared to it. Come in lower later, you've failed. Come in higher, they wonder why you lowballed them.

Titans work in ranges. "Based on what I'm seeing, we're looking at somewhere between four twenty and four fifty, depending on how we position it and what the market does in the next few weeks."

The range does three things. It gives you flexibility as the market shifts. It sets expectations without creating a hard target to miss. And it opens a conversation about positioning and strategy instead of a debate about a single number.

The same principle applies to timelines, costs, and any other variable. Ranges acknowledge uncertainty. Exact numbers create false precision that comes back to haunt you.

Work in ranges. Leave room to navigate.

. . .

The Question That Changes Everything

Early in any client conversation, ask this: "What does this move mean for your life?"

Not "What are you looking for in a home?" Not "What's your budget?" Not "When do you need to move?" Those questions gather information. This question reveals motivation.

The answer tells you everything. They're moving for a job that changes their career trajectory. They're downsizing after the kids left and reclaiming their freedom. They're buying their first home and proving to themselves they've made it. They're escaping a neighborhood that doesn't feel safe anymore.

Once you know what the move means, you connect everything back to that outcome. The house becomes a vehicle for the life change they're really after. Every feature, every decision, every dollar gets framed against what actually matters.

Ask the question. Listen to the answer. Sell the outcome they told you they wanted.

• • •

Ten Years Later

Here's what most agents miss. The value conversation doesn't end at closing.

Ten years later, your clients won't remember your marketing plan. They won't remember the staging or the open houses or the negotiation tactics. They won't remember most of the process at all.

They'll remember how you made them feel.

They'll remember that you understood what the move meant to them. That you treated their home with respect. That you guided them through something overwhelming and made it feel manageable. That you cared about their outcome, not just your commission.

That feeling is the real value you deliver. And that feeling generates referrals for decades after the transaction closes.

Sell outcomes, not features. Deliver feelings, not just results. That's the value conversation that never stops paying.

• • •

Every agent can list features. Every agent can explain what they do. That conversation leads to comparison, negotiation, and commoditization.

Titans have a different conversation. They talk about outcomes. The life the buyer is stepping into. The memories the seller is honoring. The wealth being built. The future being created.

Staging is a movie set because it sells the dream. The gazebo matters because homes hold meaning beyond market value. The wealth conversation reframes a payment into a legacy. The question about what the move means reveals the motivation behind every decision.

Stop listing what you do. Start painting what they get.

The house is never the product. The outcome is the product. Sell that.

• • •

TITAN TRUTH

No one cares what you do. Everyone cares what they get.

PILLAR 6

DISCIPLINE

CHAPTER 16

The 5 That Decide™

Daily Non-Negotiables That Shape Your Destiny

"Your calendar is a contract with your future self."

• • •

What did you do today?

Not what meetings did you sit through. Not what emails did you answer. Not what fires did you put out. What did you actually do today that moved your business forward?

Most agents can't answer that question. And here's what's worse: most agents can't tell you five productive things they have planned for today. They wake up, react to whatever comes at them, stay busy until they're tired, and call it work.

Then they wonder why they're not growing.

The difference between agents who build careers and agents who just survive isn't talent or luck or timing. It's clarity. Top producers know exactly what five things they need to do today. They knew before they got out of bed. And they'll do those five things whether they feel like it or not, whether the day cooperates or not, whether anyone notices or not.

Five things. Every day. That's the entire secret.

It sounds too simple to be true. That's why most people ignore it.

• • •

The 5 That Decide

Your success in sales comes down to five daily actions. Not fifty. Not fifteen. Five.

Lead generation. Creating new opportunities. Finding people who might need what you offer. This is the lifeblood. Without new leads, your pipeline dries up and your business dies. Every day, you generate leads or you're living on borrowed time.

Appointments. Getting face to face or voice to voice with potential clients. Leads are potential. Appointments are progress. You can't close what you can't meet. Every day, you book appointments or you're just collecting names.

Learning. Getting better at your craft. Studying scripts. Reviewing what worked. Understanding what didn't. The market evolves. Your competition improves. If you're not learning every day, you're falling behind.

Follow-up. Circling back to leads, past clients, and pending opportunities before they slip away. Most deals are won or lost in the follow-up. The fortune is in the follow-up. Every day, you follow up or you leave money on the table.

Networking. Building and nurturing your web of relationships. Meeting new people. Strengthening existing connections. Your network is your net worth. Every day, you expand it or you shrink it.

Five actions. That's it. Do them every day and you will succeed. Skip them and you won't. It's that simple. And that hard.

• • •

Why These Five

These aren't random activities I picked because they sound good. They're the five pillars that hold up every successful sales career.

Lead generation fills your pipeline. Appointments move leads forward. Learning makes you better at converting those appointments. Follow-up catches everyone who didn't convert the first time. Networking multiplies all of it by expanding your reach.

Remove any one and the system collapses. Stop generating leads and you run out of people to talk to. Stop booking appointments and leads go cold. Stop learning and you plateau. Stop following up and deals slip through the cracks. Stop networking and you become invisible.

These five work together. They feed each other. Do all five every day and you create a machine that generates momentum. Do four out of five and you create a leak that drains your progress.

• • •

The Calendar Contract

Here's where most agents fail. They agree with the concept. They understand the five. They might even write them down. Then life happens and the five become optional.

Titans treat their calendar like a contract.

When you sign a contract with a client, you don't renegotiate because you're tired. You don't cancel because something more interesting came up. You don't push it to tomorrow because today got busy. A contract is a commitment. You honor it.

Your calendar works the same way. When you block time for lead generation, that time is under contract. When you schedule follow-up calls, those calls are under contract. When you set aside thirty minutes for learning, that time is under contract.

No adjustments. No negotiations. No excuses.

Agents who treat their calendar like a suggestion end up with suggested results. Agents who treat it like a contract end up with the careers they designed.

Sign the contract with yourself every morning. Honor it every evening. That's the discipline that decides.

• • •

The Agent Who Never Cuts Corners

An agent on my team has more listings than anyone else in the brokerage. Has for the last twelve months straight. He's not the most charismatic.

Not the flashiest. Doesn't have the biggest marketing budget or the most impressive resume.

He just never cuts corners.

Every day, he does his five. Every single day. Not most days. Not the days that feel good. Every day. He generates leads when he doesn't feel like it. Follows up when he'd rather relax. Learns when he thinks he already knows enough. Networks when it would be easier to stay home.

I asked him once what his secret was. He looked at me like I'd asked a strange question. "I just do the things you taught us to do. Every day. I don't skip."

That's it. No secret system. No hidden advantage. Just relentless execution of the fundamentals while everyone else looks for shortcuts.

The people at the top of any field are rarely there because they found something others don't know. They're there because they do what others won't. Consistently. Daily. Without negotiation.

• • •

The Momentum Math

Do the math on what happens when you execute The 5 That Decide every day for a year.

Hunt for new leads every day. Stack enough days, and your pipeline overflows. Even at a modest conversion rate, consistent lead generation alone can transform your business.

Make the ask every day. Request appointments. Put yourself on the line. The more asks you make, the more opportunities you create. How many turn into clients?

Train every day. Invest focused time in yourself. Stack enough days of deliberate practice, and by year's end, you're a fundamentally different salesperson than you were at the start.

Dial every day. Pick up the phone and have real conversations. The fortune is in the follow-through. How many deals come back to life because you didn't give up?

Network every day. Expand your world intentionally. Each new connection is a potential referral source, a door to opportunity, a node that multiplies your reach.

The numbers are staggering when you stack days. And devastating when you don't. One day off doesn't feel like much. Three hundred days on feels like everything.

Ready to put this into action? Turn to the 100-Day Titan Challenge at the end of this book for the exact daily prescription.

$$\bullet \; \bullet \; \bullet$$

The Reset Trap

Here's what most people don't understand about daily discipline: momentum doesn't pause. It either builds or breaks.

When you skip a day, you don't just lose that day. You break the chain. You introduce doubt. You prove to yourself that the commitment is negotiable. And once something is negotiable, it's already lost.

The agent who skips one day finds it easier to skip the next. The excuse that worked yesterday works even better today. The muscle of discipline weakens every time you don't use it.

Meanwhile, the agent who pushes through the hard day discovers something. They prove to themselves they can. That proof becomes confidence. That confidence becomes identity. And identity is nearly impossible to break.

One day off resets the clock. Not on your streak, but on your self-belief. Protect that belief like your career depends on it. Because it does.

• • •

Feelings Are Liars

You will not feel like doing your five every day. Some days you'll be tired. Some days discouraged. Some days the market will feel impossible and the effort pointless.

Those feelings are liars.

They tell you today doesn't matter. That one day off won't hurt. That you've earned a break. That the results aren't coming anyway so why bother.

Every single one of those thoughts is a lie designed to keep you comfortable. Comfort is the enemy of growth. Feelings optimize for comfort. That makes feelings the enemy of growth.

Titans don't let feelings decide. They let commitments decide. They made the decision once, when they were thinking clearly, and they honor that decision every day regardless of how they feel.

Do the five when you feel like it. Do the five when you don't. The ones you do when you don't feel like it are the ones that actually build the career.

. . .

Becoming the Person

This chapter isn't really about five tasks. It's about who you become when you do them.

Every day you execute The 5 That Decide, you cast a vote for the person you want to be. You're telling yourself, through action, that you're the type of person who does what they committed to do. That you're disciplined. That you're serious. That your word means something, even when the only person you gave it to was yourself.

Stack enough votes and you don't have to try to be disciplined anymore. You just are. You don't have to force yourself to do the work anymore. It's just what you do. The identity becomes automatic.

That's the real prize. Not the deals you close. Not the money you make. The person you become by keeping promises to yourself day after day after day.

The 5 That Decide are the actions. But the decision they're really making is who you are.

. . .

Lead generation. Appointments. Learning. Follow-up. Networking.

Five actions. Every day. No negotiation.

Treat your calendar like a contract. Never cut corners. Do the math on momentum. Avoid the reset trap. Ignore the lies your feelings tell you. Become the person who keeps promises to themselves.

The gap between the agent who thrives and the agent who struggles isn't talent or luck or timing. It's five daily disciplines executed without exception.

These are The 5 That Decide. They're deciding your future right now. What are you going to do about it today?

• • •

TITAN TRUTH

The 5 merciless deciders of your future.

CHAPTER 17

Mastering the Wheel

Your System for Flawless Follow-Through

"The fortune is in the follow-up. The failure is in the forgetting."

• • •

You meant to call them back.

You had the conversation three weeks ago. Good connection. Real interest. They said they were thinking about selling in the spring. You said you'd check in. You wrote their name on a sticky note, or maybe you added them to your CRM with the best of intentions.

Then life happened. Other clients needed attention. Deals got busy. The sticky note got buried. The CRM task got pushed to tomorrow, then next week, then eventually marked overdue and ignored.

Six weeks later, you see the listing pop up online. Their house. With another agent's name on the sign.

That feeling in your stomach. The deal you lost wasn't lost to a better agent. It was lost to your own neglect. They didn't forget you. You forgot them.

This happens constantly. Not because agents are lazy. Not because they don't care. Because they don't have a system that forces follow-through. They rely on memory, and memory fails. They rely on motivation, and motivation fades. They rely on good intentions, and good intentions don't close deals.

The Wheel changes that. It's a system that doesn't forget, doesn't get tired, and doesn't let opportunities die from neglect.

• • •

Why We Avoid

Here's the truth no one talks about: most agents don't fail at follow-up because they forget. They fail because they avoid.

Every follow-up call is a small risk. What if they don't answer? What if they're annoyed? What if they went with someone else and you have to hear it? What if they reject you?

It's easier not to know. It's easier to tell yourself you'll call tomorrow. It's easier to let the task sit overdue than to face the possibility of disappointment.

So the call doesn't get made. And the lead goes cold. And you lose the deal not to competition, but to your own discomfort.

The Wheel solves this by removing the decision. You don't decide whether to follow up. The Wheel tells you to. Your only job is to execute. The emotional weight disappears because there's nothing to debate.

• • •

The Wheel

Picture a Ferris wheel. Every seat is a contact in your database. The wheel rotates continuously. When a seat reaches the bottom, that contact gets touched. Then the seat rises, cycles around, and comes back down later for the next touch.

Every seat stays on the wheel. Nothing gets off. Nothing gets forgotten. The wheel just keeps turning.

In practice, this means one thing: every contact in your system must have a next step. A date when they come back around. A task attached to their name. The moment a contact exists without a next step, they've fallen off the Wheel. They're in limbo. They're being forgotten.

A CRM full of contacts without next steps isn't a database. It's a graveyard. Names sitting there, decaying, while opportunities rot.

Titans don't have graveyards. They have Wheels. Every name is in motion. Every contact is scheduled for attention. Nothing sits. Nothing dies.

• • •

Drowning in Overdue

An agent on my team came to me one afternoon, overwhelmed. She was doing deals, working hard, but something was wrong. She felt behind all the time. Anxious. Like she was constantly dropping balls.

I asked her to open her CRM. She hesitated. I could see she didn't want to.

When she finally opened it, I understood why. Two hundred past-due follow-ups. Two hundred contacts she'd meant to call and hadn't. Two hundred tiny failures staring back at her every time she logged in.

She'd stopped opening the CRM because it made her feel like a failure. The longer she avoided it, the worse it got. The worse it got, the more she avoided it. A vicious cycle drowning her business while she stayed busy with everything except the thing that mattered.

We declared bankruptcy on the backlog. Cleared it. Started fresh. Then we rebuilt her system with the Wheel. Every contact got a next step. Every day, she worked only the contacts due that day. No more staring at two hundred failures. Just today's list. Just the Wheel.

Sixty days later, she had zero past-due tasks. Not because she worked more hours. Because the system didn't let things pile up. The anxiety disappeared. The avoidance stopped. Her pipeline came back to life.

She didn't become a different person. She just got a system that worked with human nature instead of against it.

• • •

Nineteen Touches

How many times do you follow up with a lead before you quit?

Most agents stop at three. Call, leave a message, maybe try once more. No response? Must not be interested. Move on.

Titans go to nineteen.

Nineteen touches over a defined cadence. Calls, texts, emails, voicemails. Spaced out. Varied in approach. Persistent without being pushy.

Why nineteen? Because most conversions happen after the fifth contact. A significant percentage happen between ten and twenty. The agent who quits at three is abandoning leads right before they would have converted.

The lead who doesn't answer on touch three might be busy. Distracted. Not ready yet. By touch twelve, their circumstances have changed. By touch fifteen, they remember you're the one who stayed in touch when everyone else gave up.

Persistence isn't annoying when it's professional. It's memorable. It's the reason they call you back six months later and say, "I'm ready now."

● ● ●

Protect Your Time

The Wheel only works if you have time to turn it.

Every hour you spend on low-value tasks is an hour stolen from follow-up. Every errand you run yourself, every lawn you mow, every task you could pay someone else to do is time you're choosing not to invest in your business.

Do the math. If your productive hourly rate is two hundred dollars and you spend two hours mowing your lawn, you didn't save the forty dollars a landscaper would cost. You lost three hundred sixty dollars. The lawn cost you four hundred dollars.

Titans keep a not-to-do list. Tasks they refuse to do because the time is worth more invested elsewhere. They delegate relentlessly. They guard their hours like they guard their money.

Every task that comes off your plate is time that goes back to the Wheel. Protect that time. It's where the money comes from.

• • •

The CRM as Memory

You cannot remember five hundred people. You can't remember who mentioned their daughter's graduation, who's thinking about selling in spring, who referred you to their neighbor last year, and who prefers texts over calls.

Your CRM can.

Titans treat their CRM as an extension of their brain. Every conversation gets noted. Every personal detail gets logged. Every commitment gets tracked. Ten seconds to type a note saves ten minutes of awkwardness later when you can't remember anything about someone you've talked to three times.

When you call a client six months later and ask how their daughter's first semester went, they think you have a remarkable memory. You don't. You have a remarkable system.

The agents who think CRM notes are busywork are the same agents who lose relationships to competitors who remember. Feed the CRM or forget the client. Those are the only options.

• • •

Follow-up is one of The 5 That Decide. The Wheel is how you execute it without fail.

Every contact needs a next step. The Wheel keeps turning. Go to nineteen before you quit. Protect your time from tasks that steal it. Let the CRM remember what you can't.

The deals you lose to poor follow-through aren't lost to better agents. They're lost to your own avoidance, your own forgetting, your own lack of system. That's the hard truth.

The good news is it's fixable. The Wheel doesn't require more talent. It doesn't require more hours. It just requires the discipline to build it and the commitment to turn it every day.

Master the Wheel. Never lose another deal to neglect.

• • •

TITAN TRUTH

The Wheel keeps turning. No contact left behind.

CHAPTER 18

Opportunity Surge

When Preparation Meets Momentum

"When everything hits at once, systems separate the Titans from the overwhelmed."

• • •

You know the feeling.

Three weeks of calls that went nowhere. Follow-ups that disappeared into silence. Open houses where no one was serious. You start wondering if you're doing something wrong.

Then Tuesday afternoon, everything changes.

A lead from two months ago calls back ready to list. While you're on that call, a text comes in from a past client with a referral. You check your email and there's a buyer inquiry on a listing you hosted last weekend. Before dinner, your phone rings again. Another referral. This one's hot.

Three weeks of nothing. Then four opportunities in four hours.

This is the surge. It's coming for every agent who does the work. The question isn't whether you'll get opportunities. The question is whether you'll be ready to capitalize when they all arrive at once.

Some agents thrive in the surge. Others drown in it. The difference isn't luck or talent. It's preparation. Systems. Triage. Communication. The infrastructure that turns chaos into closed deals.

• • •

Systems Before the Surge

The worst time to build a system is when you need it.

The agent who waits until they're overwhelmed to figure out how to handle volume is already behind. They're scrambling to create processes while opportunities slip through their fingers. Every minute spent figuring out logistics is a minute not spent serving clients.

Titans build systems during the quiet times so they're ready when things get loud.

Listing presentation ready to customize in minutes, not built from scratch every time. Follow-up templates for every scenario so responses go out fast. CRM clean and current so nothing gets lost. Transaction checklists so no step gets missed when you're juggling multiple deals. Vendor relationships already established so you're not hunting for a photographer or inspector when you need one today.

The system doesn't have to be complicated. It has to exist. When the surge hits, you're either executing a system or inventing one on the fly. One of those works. The other doesn't.

Build the machine before you need the machine. That's how you handle volume without breaking.

• • •

Resources on Standby

You can't do everything yourself during a surge. If you try, you'll drop balls. The math doesn't work. There aren't enough hours.

Titans know who they can call before they need to call them.

A transaction coordinator who can take paperwork off your plate. A showing assistant who can cover appointments when you're double-booked. A lender who responds fast and doesn't create problems. An inspector, photographer, and stager who can move on short notice. Other agents in your office who might help with an open house if you're buried.

These relationships get built during slow periods. You meet them, vet them, establish trust. Then when the surge hits and you need help immediately, you're not interviewing candidates. You're activating resources you've already lined up.

The agent with no support network handles the surge alone and misses opportunities. The agent with resources on standby delegates intelligently and captures everything.

• • •

Triage

When everything demands attention at once, you have to sort by urgency. That's triage.

Not everything is equally urgent. The buyer who wants to write an offer tonight needs you now. The seller who's thinking about listing next quarter can wait until tomorrow. The past client who's just saying hello can get a quick acknowledgment and a promise to catch up properly next week.

Triage isn't about ignoring people. It's about sequencing. Hot opportunities get handled first. Warm ones get scheduled. Cool ones get acknowledged so they know they're not forgotten.

The mistake most agents make is trying to give equal attention to everything. They answer a casual email while a hot lead waits. They spend thirty minutes on a call that could have been five while an urgent opportunity goes cold. They treat a maybe-next-year lead the same as a ready-to-sign client.

Titans assess fast. What needs me right now? What can wait an hour? What can wait until tomorrow? They make those calls instantly and act accordingly.

During a surge, you won't get to everything today. Accept that. The skill is knowing what has to happen now versus what can happen later.

$$\bullet \ \bullet \ \bullet$$

Communication That Holds

Here's what kills agents during surges: silence.

They get overwhelmed and stop communicating. Calls go unreturned for days. Emails sit in the inbox. Clients wonder what's happening with their transaction. Leads assume the agent isn't interested. Referral sources regret sending business to someone who doesn't respond.

Silence destroys trust faster than almost anything else. And it's completely preventable.

Strong communication during a surge doesn't mean long conversations with everyone. It means fast acknowledgment. A quick text: "Got your message, slammed today but I'll call you tomorrow morning." A short email: "Received this, working on it, you'll have an update by end of day." A thirty-second voicemail: "I'm with clients all day but wanted you to know I haven't forgotten you."

People don't need hours of your time. They need to know they're not being ignored. Brief, consistent communication holds relationships together when you're stretched thin.

The agents who go silent during surges lose clients they already had. The agents who communicate consistently, even briefly, keep everyone in the fold while handling the volume.

· · ·

Speed to Relationship

We talked about this earlier in the book, and it's worth repeating here because surges are where most agents forget it.

Speed to relationship beats speed to lead. Not just being first to respond, but being first to actually connect. First to understand what they need. First to feel like a human, not a pitch.

During a surge, the temptation is to cut corners on connection. Bang out quick replies. Rush through calls to get to the next one. Treat people like tasks to check off instead of relationships to build.

Resist that temptation. The agent who responds in two minutes with a generic template loses to the agent who responds in ten minutes with something personal. The agent who rushes through a call loses to the agent who's fully present for five focused minutes.

A rushed interaction that feels transactional creates a transactional relationship. A brief interaction that feels genuine creates a client who trusts you. The surge doesn't change this. If anything, it makes it more important.

Move fast. But don't sacrifice the relationship for speed. That's how you win the lead and lose the client.

• • •

The 5 Don't Stop

Here's where most agents sabotage their future during a surge: they stop doing The 5 That Decide.

They get busy with active deals and stop prospecting. They're so focused on current clients that they stop networking. They skip the learning because there's no time. They let follow-up slide because they'll get to it later. They stop asking for appointments because their schedule is full.

Three months later, the surge is over. The deals have closed. And there's nothing behind them. The pipeline is empty because they stopped filling it when things got busy.

The 5 That Decide don't take a break because you're having a good month. They're called non-negotiables for a reason. Lead generation. Appointments. Learning. Follow-up. Networking. Every day. Especially during a surge.

Yes, it's harder when you're busy. Yes, you have to protect that time more aggressively. Yes, some days it feels impossible. Do it anyway. The agents who keep doing their five during the surge are the agents who have another surge waiting when this one ends.

Being busy is not permission to abandon the activities that made you busy in the first place.

• • •

The Cost of Fumbling

Every opportunity you drop during a surge has a cost beyond the immediate commission.

The lead who doesn't get a callback goes to another agent and never comes back. The referral source who sent you business and got silence stops sending. The past client who felt ignored tells their friends. The reputation you built gets quietly undone by the opportunities you fumbled.

You worked hard to create these opportunities. You earned them through months of calls and follow-ups and relationship building. Then you lost them because you weren't ready to handle the volume.

That's the real cost. Not just the deals that slipped away. The trust that evaporated. The referrals that stopped coming. The future opportunities that never materialized because you dropped the ball when it mattered most.

Fumbling a surge doesn't just hurt today. It echoes for years.

• • •

The surge is coming. If you've been doing the work, the opportunities will arrive. Probably all at once.

When they do, you'll either be ready or you won't. You'll have systems that let you move fast, or you'll be inventing processes on the fly. You'll have resources you can activate, or you'll try to do everything alone. You'll triage effectively, or you'll give equal attention to everything and do it all poorly. You'll communicate consistently, or you'll go silent and lose trust.

The surge doesn't reward the agents who created the most opportunities. It rewards the agents who captured them. The ones with systems in place. Resources on standby. The discipline to triage. The communication skills to hold relationships together under pressure.

Build the infrastructure now. The flood is coming. Be ready to capture it.

• • •

TITAN TRUTH

Systems, triage, communication. That's how you capture the surge.

INNER CIRCLE

CHAPTER 19

Referrals on Repeat

The Multiplier Every Closer Needs

"Train your referrers how to refer."

• • •

Listen for the word.

When a client introduces you to someone and says "This is our agent," something has shifted. Not my agent. Not the agent. Our agent. That word carries weight. You've moved from vendor to trusted advisor. From someone who did a job to someone who's part of their story.

Your name now lives in their phone next to their mechanic, doctor, and attorney. When someone asks "Do you know a good agent?", they don't hesitate. Your name is the answer.

That's the goal. Becoming the name people say out loud when someone they care about needs help.

But here's what most agents miss: referrals don't just happen because you did a good job. They happen because you built a system that makes referring you easy, natural, and repeatable.

• • •

Why Referrals Are Different

Every lead has a cost. Money, time, energy, or all three. You pay for attention. You work to earn trust. You start every relationship from zero.

Referrals arrive different. Pre-warmed. Someone already vouched for you. The trust that takes weeks to build with a cold lead exists from the first conversation with a referred one.

Referrals close faster because doubt is lower. Higher quality because someone filtered for fit. More loyal because they didn't find you through an ad. They found you through someone they trust.

But here's the deeper truth: when someone refers you, they're lending you their reputation. They're telling their friend, "I trust this person with the biggest financial decision of your life." That's not a favor given lightly. And it's not one you should leave to chance.

Titans don't wait for referrals to happen. They create systems that make referrals inevitable.

• • •

Train Your Referrers

Most agents wait passively for referrals. Someone mentions they know a person thinking about buying, and the agent says "Have them give me a call." Then they wait. And wait. The referral never comes because the connection never happened.

Titans train their referrers how to refer.

When someone mentions a friend or family member who might need help, don't say "Have them call me." Say "What's their number? I'll reach out directly." Or "Can you text me their contact info? I'd love to help."

You're not being pushy. You're being professional. You're taking the burden off your client to play middleman. You're controlling the referral instead of hoping it happens.

The difference between "have them call me" and "what's their number" is the difference between referrals that evaporate and referrals that convert. One puts the work on someone else. The other puts it where it belongs: on you.

Train your people. Make it easy for them. Take control of the connection.

• • •

The Text Chain

Here's a technique that turns warm referrals into hot ones.

When a client gives you a referral's contact info, don't call out of the blue. Ask your client to send a text introduction first. Something simple: "Hey, I'm connecting you with my agent. She's amazing. She's going to reach out."

Then have them add you to the thread. Now when you reach out, the referral sees the history. They see their friend vouching for you. They see the relationship is real, not just a cold call claiming to be a referral.

That text chain does more for your credibility than anything you could say yourself. It's proof. The referral sees their trusted friend recommending you in writing. The conversation starts on completely different footing.

Make the referral visible. Let them see the handoff. It transforms a maybe into a yes before you say hello.

• • •

Two in a Row

An agent on my team had a buyer consultation scheduled. Standard appointment.

The client showed up and brought her sister. "She's thinking about buying too. Mind if she sits in?"

The agent didn't mind. Ran the consultation the same way she always did. Professional. Thorough. Answered every question. Set clear expectations. By the end, both sisters signed. Two clients from one appointment.

That's what happens when you run consultations at a level worth sharing. The first sister was so confident she brought family along. The referral didn't happen after the transaction. It happened during the process because the process itself was referable.

Your clients talk about you. They tell people what you did, how you handled things, what the experience was like. Make sure the story they're telling makes people want to meet you.

• • •

Give Them Something to Say

Your clients do your marketing for you. They just need material.

When you do something memorable, it becomes a story they tell. "My agent took my vacant home and made it look professionally staged." "She remembered my kids' names six months later." "He showed up to the inspection even though he didn't have to." "She talked me off the ledge when I was panicking about the appraisal."

These aren't just nice moments. They're referral fuel. The specific details that surface when someone asks "Do you know a good agent?" Your client doesn't say "Yeah, she was professional." They say "Let me tell you what she did."

Create moments worth talking about. Go beyond expected. Do the thing that makes them say "You won't believe what my agent did." That story gets told at dinner parties, in group texts, at family gatherings.

The best referral marketing isn't marketing at all. It's being so good your clients can't stop talking about you.

• • •

The Referral Loop

An agent I know built a relationship with a contractor. Every time she closed a deal, she'd recommend him for any work the new homeowner needed. He did good work, made her look good, clients were happy.

Then something interesting started happening. The contractor began referring her back. He'd be on a job, homeowner would mention thinking about selling, and he'd say "I know the perfect agent" and make the introduction.

Same thing happened with a blacktop company. Refer them business, they refer business back. The loop feeds itself.

This isn't transactional. It's relational. A network of people who send business to each other because they trust each other's work. The more you give, the more comes back. The loop expands.

Build referral loops with vendors and professionals you trust. Multiplies everyone's business while serving clients better. That's how networks become net worth.

• • •

Close the Loop

When someone refers you, they're putting their reputation on the line. They told their friend, "This person is worth your trust." If you drop the ball, they look bad. If you never follow up, they look bad. If the experience is mediocre, they look bad.

Titans close the loop.

The moment you receive a referral, thank the person who sent it. Not a week later. That day. A quick text: "Just connected with Sarah. Thank you for thinking of me." That acknowledgment tells them you took it seriously.

Keep them updated. "We found Sarah the perfect place. Closing next month." They want to know their recommendation paid off. They want to feel like they helped their friend.

After closing, circle back again. "Sarah is all moved in. She's thrilled. That never happens without you making the introduction." Now they feel like part of the success. Now they're looking for the next person to send your way.

The referrer who never hears back stops referring. The referrer who gets thanked, updated, and appreciated becomes a referral machine. Close the loop every time.

• • •

Stay in Touch or Stay Forgotten

We talked about the Wheel earlier in this book. Every contact on a system that keeps turning. No one falls through the cracks. That system isn't just for active leads. It's how you stay present with past clients who could refer you for years.

The closing isn't the end. It's the beginning of a referral relationship that could last decades. But only if you stay in touch.

Most agents disappear after closing. Move on to the next deal and forget the client they just served. Eighteen months later, that client's coworker asks if they know a good agent. The client can barely remember your name. The referral goes to whoever stayed present.

Your past clients belong on the Wheel just like your prospects. Check-ins when there's nothing to sell. Quick texts just to say hello. The touches don't have to be complicated. They just have to happen.

The agent who stays top of mind gets the referral. The agent who disappears gets forgotten. Put your past clients on the Wheel and keep it turning.

• • •

Referrals aren't luck. They're the result of being worth referring and making it easy to refer you.

Train your referrers. Control the connection. Use the text chain. Create moments worth talking about. Build referral loops with trusted vendors. Close the loop every time. Keep past clients on the Wheel.

Do these things consistently and you stop chasing leads. They start coming to you. Pre-warmed. Pre-trusted. Ready to work with the agent their friend couldn't stop talking about.

Become the name people say out loud. Then give them every reason to keep saying it.

• • •

TITAN TRUTH

Make referring you the easiest thing your clients ever do.

CHAPTER 20

Your Network Is Your Net Worth

How Elite Connectors Dominate Their Markets

"Sales is a contact sport."

• • •

Think about the last wedding you attended.

Count the guests. Family, friends, coworkers, neighbors. The people that couple has built relationships with over a lifetime. On average, that's somewhere between one hundred fifty and two hundred people.

Now think about your own life. The people you'd invite to a major event. Family. Friends from different chapters. Colleagues past and present. Neighbors. Parents you've met through your kids. People from your gym, your church, your community groups.

You know one hundred fifty to two hundred people. So does everyone else.

That's the math that changes everything. Every person you build a real relationship with isn't just one potential client. They're a gateway to one hundred fifty more. Every connection compounds. Every relationship multiplies.

Your network is your net worth. Not a cliché. Math.

• • •

A Contact Sport

Sales is a contact sport. You have to make contact to play.

Not digital contact. Not social media likes and comments. Real contact. Conversations. Coffees. Phone calls. Face-to-face interactions where you're actually present.

Agents who sit behind screens wondering why their phone doesn't ring are losing to agents out in the world making contact. Every day. With intention. Building relationships that turn into business.

You can't network from your couch. Can't build relationships through email alone. You have to show up. Shake hands. Look people in the eye. Have conversations that aren't about selling anything.

The more contact you make, the larger your network grows. The larger your network grows, the more opportunities find you. Not complicated. Just work most people aren't willing to do.

• • •

The Connection Compass

Earlier in this book, we introduced the Connection Compass, the NEWS system for turning contacts into real connections. Next, Energy, Work, Soil. Four directions that point you toward a real relationship.

That system doesn't just apply to your existing database. It applies to everyone you meet.

Every new conversation is a chance to gather NEWS. The person at the networking event. The parent at your kid's game. The vendor you're working with for the first time. Ask good questions. Listen. Capture it in your CRM.

When you know someone's NEWS, your follow-up becomes personal. Your conversations have depth. You're not just another salesperson in their contacts. You're someone who actually knows them.

The more NEWS you gather, the better you can serve people when the moment is right. Information is opportunity.

• • •

The Coffee Strategy

An agent I work with built a career-changing relationship over coffee.

He reached out to a real estate attorney in town. Not to pitch anything. Just to learn. "I'd love to understand your side of the business better. Can I buy you a coffee?"

They met. The agent asked questions about what goes wrong in transactions, what makes an agent easy to work with, what the attorney wishes agents understood. Genuine curiosity. No agenda.

That coffee turned into a relationship. The attorney started recommending him to clients who needed an agent. The agent referred clients who needed legal help. Both businesses grew because two people took an hour to connect.

The coffee strategy works with anyone. Lenders. Inspectors. Financial advisors. Other agents in complementary markets. Anyone whose world intersects with yours. Reach out. Learn their business. Build the relationship before you need it.

One coffee. One conversation. One relationship that pays dividends for years.

• • •

Create Your Own Opportunities

Don't wait for networking events to come to you. Create them.

Organize a coffee meetup for young professionals. Host a lunch for local business owners. Put together a happy hour for people in related industries. You don't need permission. Don't need a big budget. Just send invitations and pick a time and place.

When you organize the event, you're positioned as the connector. Everyone there knows you brought them together. That's a different position than being another face in the crowd at someone else's event.

The agent who creates networking opportunities is remembered. The agent who just shows up is forgotten. Be the one who makes things happen. Build the room instead of walking into it.

Titans don't wait for opportunity. They create the conditions where opportunity finds them.

• • •

The Power of Solving Problems

A client came to me with a problem that had nothing to do with real estate. Credit score sitting at 600. They wanted to buy a house but couldn't qualify for financing. Most agents would have said "Come back when your credit is fixed."

I made a call. Connected them with someone in my network who specializes in credit repair. Three weeks later, their score was 740. Three weeks. They qualified. They bought. They've sent me four referrals since. Because I solved a problem I didn't have to solve.

That's what a network does. It lets you solve problems beyond your expertise. You become the person who knows a person. The one who makes things happen. The one people call when they don't know who else to call.

Build a network of people who are great at what they do. Connect people with problems to people with solutions. That's how you become indispensable.

• • •

Become the Connector

The most valuable person in any room isn't the one with the most knowledge. It's the one who connects people.

When you introduce two people who can help each other, you create value that didn't exist before. The contractor who meets the flipper. The financial advisor who meets the young couple. The business owner who meets the commercial landlord. You made that happen. They'll both remember.

Titans look for connection opportunities constantly. In every conversation, they're thinking: who else would benefit from knowing this person? Then they make the introduction. Not for credit. Not for commission. Just because connecting people is what they do.

Over time, this positions you differently. You're not just an agent. You're a resource. The person who knows everyone. The one people call when they need anything, even if it has nothing to do with real estate.

The more you connect others, the more connected you become. The more valuable you make your network to others, the more valuable your network becomes to you.

• • •

From Contact to Connection

There's a difference between knowing someone and being known by them.

You can have a thousand contacts in your phone. A database full of names. That's not a network. That's a list. A network is built on connection. People who actually know you. People who would take your call. People who trust you enough to stake their reputation on recommending you.

The question isn't how many people you know. It's how many would vouch for you. How many would say your name when someone asks for a recommendation. How many consider you part of their trusted circle.

Contacts are collected. Connections are cultivated. One is a number. The other is an asset that compounds over time.

Stop counting contacts. Start building connections.

• • •

Your network is your net worth. Every person you know is a gateway to one hundred fifty more. Every relationship compounds. Every connection multiplies.

Make contact. Gather the NEWS. Use the coffee strategy. Create your own opportunities. Build relationships that solve problems beyond your expertise. Become the connector. Turn contacts into connections.

Agents who struggle are usually isolated. Trying to build a business alone. Agents who thrive are connected. They've built a web of relationships that feeds them opportunities, solves problems, multiplies their reach.

Build the network. Watch it build your business.

• • •

TITAN TRUTH

Every person you know is a gateway to one hundred fifty more.

CHAPTER 21

The Titan's Inner Circle

Your Circle Is Your Ceiling

"Titans don't rise alone. They rise with the right people beside them."

• • •

You've spent this book learning how to build outward.

How to find clients. How to serve them. How to build systems that create consistency. How to develop skills that command respect. How to nurture relationships that generate referrals. How to construct a network that feeds your business for life.

All of it points outward. Toward the people you serve. The business you're building. The legacy you're creating.

But one question remains.

Who's building you?

Who pushes you when you want to coast? Who tells you the truth when you're slipping? Who believes in you when you've stopped believing in yourself? Who do you call when the deal falls apart, when the client fires you, when the year isn't going the way you planned?

The Titan's Inner Circle. The people who make you better. The ones who won't let you stay small.

This chapter ties everything together. Because you can have all the systems and skills and strategies in the world, but if you're trying to do this alone, you'll eventually break.

• • •

The Lonely Agent

Real estate is one of the loneliest professions on earth.

You work for yourself. Set your own schedule. Win alone and lose alone. No team in the break room celebrating your victory. No manager pulling you aside after a tough loss. Just you, your phone, and the next thing on your list.

Most agents never talk about this. They post wins on social media. Smile at the closing table. Pretend everything is fine. But behind the scenes, they're drowning. No one to talk to. No one who understands. No one in their corner.

The lonely agent burns out. Makes the same mistakes year after year because no one catches them. Plateaus because no one pushes them higher. Quits, not because the business beat them, but because the isolation did.

Titans refuse to operate this way. The lone wolf doesn't survive. The wolf with a pack does.

. . .

The Five Seats

Your inner circle needs five seats filled. Not five hundred. Five.

The Mentor. Someone who's been where you're going. Who's already made the mistakes you're about to make. Who sees around corners you can't see yet. The mentor doesn't do the work for you. They illuminate the path.

The Peer. Someone in the arena with you. Fighting the same fights. Facing the same challenges. Not ahead of you, not behind you, beside you. The peer understands what you're going through because they're going through it too.

The Accountability Partner. Someone who won't let you lie to yourself. Who asks the hard questions. Who calls you out when you're making excuses. The accountability partner doesn't accept your stories. They demand your results.

The Believer. Someone who sees the version of you that you can't always see. Who reminds you of your potential when you've forgotten it. Who refuses to let you quit. The believer holds the vision when you've lost sight of it.

The Student. Someone you're pouring into. Coming up behind you. Teaching forces clarity. Mentoring cements what you've learned. The student keeps you sharp and reminds you how far you've come.

Five seats. Some people might fill more than one. But if any seat stays empty too long, you'll feel it. The circle won't be complete.

• • •

Finding Your People

Your inner circle won't find you. You have to find them.

Look for people playing at a level you respect. Not just production numbers, character, work ethic, how they treat people when no one's watching. Success without integrity isn't worth emulating.

Start with proximity. Your brokerage. Your market. Industry events. Masterminds. Coaching programs. The people you admire are closer than you think. You just haven't reached out.

Then reach out. Not with an ask. With value. "I've watched how you run your business. I'd love to learn more. Can I buy you lunch?" Most people never ask. The ones who do stand out.

Not everyone will say yes. That's fine. You're not looking for everyone. You're looking for the right five. One mentor. One peer. One accountability partner. One believer. One student. That's all it takes to change everything.

Finding your people requires initiative. Keeping them requires intention.

• • •

The Two-Way Street

The inner circle isn't a fan club. Not a group of people who exist to serve you. It's a two-way street. You get what you give.

When your peer has a bad month, you're there. When your mentor needs something you can provide, you provide it. When your accountability partner is slipping, you call them out the same way they call you out. The circle only works if everyone invests in everyone else.

Selfishness kills inner circles. The person who only takes eventually gets cut off. The person who only shows up when they need something stops getting invitations. The person who disappears when others need them finds themselves alone.

Show up for your people. Celebrate their wins like your own. Carry their burdens when they're too heavy. Be the person they can count on, and they'll be the people you can count on.

You don't just need an inner circle. You need to be someone worthy of being in someone else's.

· · ·

The Accountability Factor

The most valuable people in your circle are often the ones who make you uncomfortable.

Not mean. Not cruel. Honest. The ones who ask how many calls you actually made this week. Who don't let you blame the market when you didn't do the work. Who remind you of the commitment you made when you're looking for an excuse to break it.

Most people surround themselves with comfort. Friends who nod along. Family who tells them what they want to hear. Colleagues who don't push back. Feels nice. But comfort doesn't create growth.

Titans invite accountability. They want people who will challenge them. Who see through the excuses. Who hold them to a higher standard than they'd hold themselves.

Find people who care enough to be honest with you. Then listen when they speak. The feedback that stings most is usually the feedback you need most.

Comfort is the enemy of growth. Accountability is the antidote.

• • •

Protecting Your Circle

Not everyone deserves a seat.

Some people drain energy instead of creating it. Tear down instead of building up. Some are so committed to their own negativity they'll poison anyone who gets too close.

Titans protect their circle fiercely. They're intentional about who gets access. They don't let geography or history or obligation determine who influences them. Blood doesn't guarantee a seat. Tenure doesn't guarantee a seat. Only alignment and mutual investment guarantee a seat.

This isn't about being cold. It's about being clear. You can love people and still recognize they're not right for your inner circle. You can care about someone and still create distance when their presence makes you worse instead of better.

Audit your circle regularly. Who energizes you? Who drains you? Who pushes you forward? Who holds you back? The answers matter more than you think.

You become who you surround yourself with. Choose carefully.

• • •

The Circle That Changes Everything

I've watched agents transform when they finally build their circle.

Agents stuck for years break through because a mentor showed them what they couldn't see. Agents burning out find renewed energy because a peer reminded them they weren't alone. Agents making the same mistakes finally change because an accountability partner refused to let them keep lying to themselves.

The tactics in this book will make you better. The systems will make you consistent. The skills will make you valuable. But the circle? The circle makes everything else sustainable.

Because there will be days when you don't want to do the work. Days when the market feels impossible. Days when you question whether any of this is worth it. On those days, your inner circle carries you. They remind you why you started. Push you when you want to stop. Hold you together when you're falling apart.

You can build a business alone. You can't build a legacy alone.

• • •

The pages are running out. But what you're building is just getting started.

You have the mindset now. The systems. The skills. The relationships. Everything you need to become what most salespeople only dream about.

But none of it matters if you try to do this alone.

Find your mentor. Your peer. Your accountability partner. Your believer. Your student. Fill the five seats. Build the circle that builds you.

Then go do the work. Make the calls. Have the conversations. Run the systems. Develop the skills. Nurture the relationships. Day after day, week after week, year after year.

And when you look back, years from now, with a business that runs, a reputation that precedes you, and a life you're proud of, you'll know the truth.

You didn't do it alone. And that's exactly why you made it.

• • •

TITAN TRUTH

The Titan doesn't rise alone.

UNBREAKABLE

Pillar 1 built the Titan within. Pillar 8 makes you unbreakable to the world.

CHAPTER 22

The Rejection-Proof Mind

How to Take a Thousand "No's" Without Breaking

" Spray Teflon on your shoulders. Nothing sticks."

• • •

Nobody quits this business because of skill.

After watching hundreds of agents come through my brokerage, some who thrived, some who vanished, I can tell you with certainty: The agents who leave rarely leave because they couldn't learn the scripts. They don't leave because they couldn't master the market. They don't leave because they lacked the intelligence or the work ethic.

They leave because rejection eroded them.

Slowly. Silently. One "no" at a time. Until the morning comes when they can't pick up the phone. Can't make themselves walk into another listing appointment. Can't stomach the thought of hearing one more person say they've decided to go with someone else.

It's death by a thousand cuts.

And here's what makes it insidious: It doesn't feel like erosion while it's happening. It feels like a bad day. Then a bad week. Then a month where nothing seems to work. Then a creeping suspicion that maybe this business isn't for them. Then a quiet exit, disguised as a "career pivot" or "taking a break."

The rejection won.

This chapter is your armor.

• • •

The Pain Is Real

Before we talk about overcoming rejection, let's acknowledge something most sales trainers skip over: The pain is real.

Research shows that social rejection activates the same regions of the brain associated with physical pain, the anterior cingulate cortex and the anterior insula. Studies have found that your brain processes rejection the same way it processes a punch to the gut.

Your brain processes rejection the same way it processes a punch to the gut.

This isn't weakness. It's wiring. For hundreds of thousands of years, being rejected by the tribe meant death. Exile from the group meant exposure to predators, starvation, elimination from the gene pool. Your ancestors who felt rejection deeply and course-corrected? They survived. The ones who shrugged it off? They got eaten.

You are the descendant of people who took rejection seriously.

So when you hang up the phone after someone curses you out, and your chest tightens, and your mood darkens, and part of you wants to crawl under your desk, that's not a character flaw. That's evolution. Your brain is trying to protect you from what it perceives as a survival threat.

The problem is, your brain can't distinguish between rejection from a stranger on a cold call and rejection from your tribe. It fires the same alarm either way. And if you don't learn to override that alarm, it will drive you out of this business.

Titans don't feel rejection less. They've learned to process it differently.

That processing starts with a single distinction.

. . .

The First Shift: They're Not Rejecting You

Here's the reframe that changes everything:

When a prospect says no, they are rejecting the situation. They are not rejecting you.

You make it about yourself because you're involved in the process. But step back for a moment. What are they actually saying no to?

They're saying no to talking on the phone right now. They're saying no to thinking about real estate today. They're saying no to the timing, the offer, the approach, the interruption. They're saying no to a hundred things that have nothing to do with you as a human being.

They don't know you. They've spent thirty seconds with your voice. They have no idea about your character, your capabilities, your worth as a person. How could they be rejecting that? They're rejecting a situation.

An agent I trained was working as an ISA before he became licensed. Phone calls all day, every day. Getting cursed out, hung up on, told to never call again. Hundreds of rejections.

"Eventually," he told the team, "after doing it so many times and hearing it, you kind of just laugh at it."

That's not because he became numb. It's because he finally understood: These people weren't rejecting him. They didn't know him. They were rejecting the interruption to their Tuesday afternoon. That's it.

When you internalize this distinction, situation versus self, something shifts. The rejection stops feeling like an indictment of your worth and starts feeling like what it actually is: information about timing and circumstances.

$$\bullet \ \bullet \ \bullet$$

The Bank Account of Seconds

There are 86,400 seconds in every day.

Imagine that number as a bank account. Every morning, you wake up with a fresh deposit: 86,400 seconds to spend however you choose.

Now imagine someone says something mean to you on a phone call. It takes ten seconds. Maybe thirty, if they're really going off.

Ask yourself: If thirty dollars of your money was counterfeit, would you throw away the other 86,370?

Of course not. That would be insane.

But that's exactly what happens when you let one bad phone call ruin your entire day. You take thirty seconds of negativity and let it poison the remaining 86,370. You hand that person power over your hours, your mood, your productivity, all because of half a minute they've already forgotten about.

Titans guard their seconds.

When someone gives you ten seconds of garbage, you don't owe them the next ten hours of your mental energy. Take the hit. Acknowledge it happened. Then move on. The day is still full of seconds that belong to you.

The person who cursed you out is already thinking about something else. Why are you still thinking about them?

• • •

The Second Shift: Rejection as Data

This is where most "positive thinking" advice fails: It tells you to ignore rejection. Let it bounce off. Don't think about it.

That's incomplete.

You don't want to let rejection roll off so completely that you learn nothing. Every rejection contains data. The question is whether you're mining it correctly.

When someone says no, the first thing you should ask yourself is: What specifically did they say no to?

Not "they rejected me." That's too vague, too personal. Get specific. What was the actual objection? What was the moment they pulled back? What words triggered the resistance?

Maybe your opening was too aggressive. Maybe you hit them at the wrong time. Maybe your pacing was off. Maybe they'd just gotten off a bad call with someone else, and you caught the residual frustration. Maybe, and this is important, maybe you did everything right and they still weren't ready.

All of that is data. All of it is useful. None of it is a judgment on your worth as a person.

Those who improve are the ones who autopsy their rejections. Not to beat themselves up, that's the trap, but to extract the lesson. What can I adjust? What could I say differently? Was there a signal I missed?

Then, and this is crucial, you take the lesson and release the emotion.

The data stays. The sting goes.

Rejection as data, not as verdict. That's the shift.

• • •

The Math That Sets You Free

Early in my career, I figured out something that changed my relationship with rejection forever.

I reverse-engineered my numbers. Tracked everything. Discovered that, on average, I needed to make about seventy phone calls to book one appointment. And I knew what my average appointment was worth in terms of eventual commission.

So I did the math. Every single phone call I made was worth approximately forty dollars. Not forty dollars if they said yes. Forty dollars regardless of outcome. The math worked out over time. Some calls became nothing. Some became massive deals. But averaged across all of them, every dial was worth forty bucks.

Someone curses me out? I just made forty dollars. Someone hangs up? Forty dollars. Someone isn't interested? Forty dollars. Someone tells me I'm the tenth agent to call them today and they're sick of it? Forty dollars, my friend. Thank you for the contribution.

The outcome of any individual call stopped mattering. I wasn't prospecting for yeses anymore. I was prospecting for value, and every call had value.

Do your own math. Figure out what each activity is worth to you over time. Then watch how differently you feel when the rejection comes. It's not a loss anymore. It's a payment.

I don't know about you, but someone can be pretty rude to me for forty dollars. I can handle that all day.

...

The Third Shift: Build the Callus

Your fingers don't hurt after a thousand guitar chords.

When you first pick up the instrument, the strings bite into soft flesh. Every practice session leaves marks, tenderness, frustration. But keep playing. Day after day, week after week. Something changes. The skin hardens. Calluses form. What once caused pain becomes unremarkable.

Your mind builds calluses the same way.

Agents who can't handle rejection usually aren't avoiding it because it hurts. They're avoiding the volume of rejection that would build their calluses.

Ten calls a day keeps you fragile. A hundred calls a day makes you bulletproof.

This isn't about masochism. It's about exposure. The more rejection you experience, the less any individual rejection registers. Your threshold rises. What once felt like a gut punch becomes a minor annoyance, then background noise, then something you barely notice at all.

One of the toughest agents I've ever known told me his secret: "When I started, I deliberately went after the hardest calls first. The ones everyone else was afraid of. I figured if I was going to get rejected, I might as well get rejected hard and fast. Get it over with."

He wasn't trying to succeed with those calls. He was trying to desensitize himself to failure. And it worked. Within months, he could handle anything. The calls that made other agents crumble barely registered for him.

Calluses come from playing, not avoiding.

• • •

The Reset Ritual

Even with the right mindset, rejection lands. You're human. Some calls will get to you. Some losses will sting.

The key isn't to not feel it. The key is to not carry it.

Titans develop what I call a Reset Ritual, a deliberate practice that draws a hard line between what just happened and what happens next.

For some people, it's physical. A walk around the block. Ten pushups. Something that discharges the nervous energy and resets the body. Movement changes chemistry, and chemistry changes mood.

For others, it's verbal. Speaking out loud: "That was one call out of the five hundred I'm making this month. Noted. Moving on." Hearing yourself acknowledge and dismiss it makes it real. You're not pretending it didn't happen. You're choosing not to let it metastasize.

For others, it's musical. A song that shifts your energy. Something that floods the brain with a different set of associations and emotions. Three minutes of the right track can completely reset your state.

For others, it's mathematical. Reminding yourself of the forty-dollar value. Saying "That was a forty-dollar call. Next forty-dollar call coming up." Reframing the experience in terms of value rather than judgment.

The ritual itself doesn't matter. Having one does.

Without a reset ritual, rejections accumulate. They stack on top of each other. Each one becomes evidence for a story you don't want to be telling yourself. Ten rejections become "nobody wants to work with me." Twenty become "I'm bad at this." Fifty become "maybe I should quit."

With a reset ritual, each rejection stays isolated. A single event. Processed and released. No accumulation. No compounding. No erosion.

Build your ritual. Use it religiously. The agents who last are the ones who've mastered the reset.

• • •

The Sorry for Your Loss Technique

A top producer on my team shared a technique he learned from another high performer.

Every time someone rejected this agent, he would mentally, and sometimes literally, send them a "sorry for your loss" message in his mind.

Not sorry for his own loss.

Sorry for theirs.

Because if they were rejecting him, they were missing out on the best agent they could have worked with. Their loss. Not his.

This sounds arrogant until you understand what it's actually doing. It's a complete inversion of the rejection narrative. Instead of "they rejected me because I'm not good enough," it becomes "they rejected me because they don't realize how good I am yet."

Same event. Completely different story. And the story you tell yourself determines the emotional impact.

Try it sometime. When someone says no, genuinely think: That's too bad for them. They would have been well-served. Their loss.

You're not deluding yourself. If you're reading this book, if you're doing the work, if you're committed to becoming a Titan, you genuinely are a better choice than most agents out there. When someone rejects you, they are losing something, whether they know it or not.

Feel sorry for them. Then move on.

• • •

The Fuel Conversion

Most books won't tell you this: Some rejections should stay with you.

Not as wounds. As fuel.

One of my team members admitted that rejections from five, even ten years ago still come up in his mind sometimes. Clients who fired him. Deals that fell apart. Moments where he felt dismissed or underestimated.

But here's how he uses them: "I don't want to feel like that again."

Those memories aren't dragging him down. They're pushing him forward. Every time one of those old rejections surfaces, it becomes motivation. A reminder of why he shows up prepared. Why he never coasts. Why he fights for every deal like his reputation depends on it, because it does.

The difference between carrying rejection and converting it to fuel is simple: Are you replaying the wound, or are you channeling the lesson?

Replaying the wound sounds like: "I can't believe they did that to me. I'm so angry. That was so unfair."

Channeling the lesson sounds like: "I remember how that felt. I never want to give anyone that opening again. I'm going to be so good they can't dismiss me."

Same memory. Two completely different outcomes based on how you hold it. One keeps you stuck. The other propels you forward. You get to choose which relationship you have with your past rejections. Choose fuel.

• • •

The Line He Wouldn't Cross

Let me tell you about an agent on my team who got fired by a client.

They'd been working together for months. Good relationship, or so he thought. Then the clients decided they wanted to make an unreasonable request to the sellers, demanding replacement of the furnace, water heater, and A/C unit when there was nothing wrong with any of them. My agent refused to present a demand he knew would blow up the deal and make his clients look unreasonable.

They fired him.

Walked out. Found another agent. Went shopping for someone who would tell them what they wanted to hear.

That rejection stung. He'd done the right thing, protected them from their own bad instincts, and gotten punished for it.

He never heard from them again. Maybe they found an agent who played along. Maybe they blew up that deal too. He doesn't know, and he stopped wondering.

What he does know is this: he kept his standards. He didn't bend to save a commission. He didn't compromise his judgement to avoid an uncomfortable goodbye. And everyclient he's worked with since has gotten the same version of him; honest, direct, willing to lose the deal to protect them from themselves.

That rejection wasn't a failure. It was a filter. And it proved something to himself: his standards weren't for sale.

You can't control whether clients are ready. You can control whether you hold your standards. When you hold them, sometimes you lose in the short term. But those who bend to avoid rejection end up losing something worse: their reputation and their self-respect.

• • •

The Customer Appreciation Event Reset

When rejection has beaten you down, when your confidence is shaky, when you're starting to wonder if you're actually good at this, there's a reset button more powerful than any technique I've mentioned.

Throw a customer appreciation event.

Invite everyone who's ever worked with you. Past clients, current clients, anyone who's been in your orbit. Get them in a room together.

Then watch what happens.

They'll start talking to each other. About you. About the experience of working with you. About the things you did that mattered to them. About why they'd recommend you to anyone who asked.

You don't have to prompt it. Just create the environment and let it unfold.

I've seen agents completely transform their relationship with themselves after one of these events. All the rejection that had accumulated, all the doubt that had crept in, all the stories about not being good enough, dissolved in an afternoon of watching real people genuinely appreciate what they do.

That's not delusion. That's data. Real evidence from real people who actually know your work. And it carries weight that no affirmation can match.

...

The Actions, Not the Results

This is the final shift, and it might be the most important:

Stop focusing on results. Focus on actions.

If you made a hundred calls today and didn't book a single appointment, here's the wrong response: "I'm a terrible salesperson. This isn't working. I should give up."

Here's the right response: "I made a hundred calls today. No other agent in my office did that. I'm going to be incredibly successful."

Both responses are about the same day. Same events. Same outcomes. But one response lets rejection in, and one keeps it out.

Results are lagging indicators. They show up weeks or months after the work that produced them. If you judge yourself by today's results, you're always looking at the past. And if the past looks bad, you'll feel bad, even if you just planted the seeds for a record-breaking month.

Actions are leading indicators. They predict where you're going, not where you've been. If you judge yourself by today's actions, you're looking at the future. And if you did the work today, you know the results are coming, even if they haven't arrived yet.

Focus on actions. Do the work. Trust that results follow inputs. They always do. They always have. They always will.

• • •

The Accumulation Trap

Understand this about rejection:

It almost never kills in a single blow. It kills through accumulation.

One bad call doesn't take anyone out. One lost listing doesn't end a career. One client who fires you doesn't destroy your confidence.

But one hundred bad calls that you never properly processed? Ten lost listings that you internalized as evidence of your inadequacy? A pattern of clients leaving that you've woven into a story about your fundamental unworthiness?

That accumulation destroys careers.

Titans don't let rejection accumulate. They process each one as it comes. Extract the lesson. Execute the reset. Return to baseline before the next one arrives.

It's not that they feel rejection less. It's that they don't let it compound. They keep the account balanced. They don't carry yesterday's rejection into today's calls.

You have my permission to feel it when it happens. Feel the sting. Acknowledge the disappointment. You're human.

But you do not have permission to carry it. You do not have permission to stack it. You do not have permission to let it compound into a weight that crushes your career.

Feel it. Process it. Release it. Reset. Move forward.

. . .

So what separates the agents who last?

The agents who survive this business long enough to thrive aren't the ones who avoid rejection. They're the ones who've learned to process it at a speed that prevents accumulation.

- They understand that rejection targets situations, not selves.

- They protect their bank account of seconds.

- They mine rejection for data while releasing the emotion.

- They do the math that makes each call valuable regardless of outcome.

- They build calluses through deliberate volume.

- They develop reset rituals that prevent compounding.

- They convert old rejections into fuel instead of wounds.

- They focus on actions they control, not results they can't.

And when it all gets too heavy, they surround themselves with people who actually know their worth, the clients they've served, the relationships they've built, the evidence that contradicts every doubt the rejection was trying to plant.

You will be rejected in this business. Not might be. Will be. Thousands of times over your career. That's the price of admission.

The question isn't how to avoid the rejection. The question is how to make yourself rejection-proof.

Now you're armed.

. . .

TITAN TRUTH

The wound is real. The story is optional.

CHAPTER 23

The Authority Advantage

Becoming the Obvious Choice Before You Walk in the Room

" Perception becomes reality. Control the perception."

• • •

When do you think they actually decide to hire you?

Most agents believe it happens during the listing presentation. They think the PowerPoint matters. The market analysis matters. The commission conversation matters. They prepare their pitch like it's a job interview, hoping to win the client over with credentials and charm.

They're wrong.

In most cases, the decision is made before you walk through the door.

Think about it. By the time a seller invites you to their kitchen table, they've already Googled your name. They've checked your reviews. They've scrolled your social media. They've asked their neighbor who sold their house last year. They've formed an impression, an expectation, a lean.

The listing presentation doesn't determine whether you get hired. It determines whether you lose a decision that was already made in your favor.

If you walk in with authority, you're there to confirm what they already believe: that you're the right choice. All you have to do is not blow it.

If you walk in without authority, you're there to convince. To prove. To overcome the gap between who you are and who they hoped you'd be. That's a much harder game.

This chapter is about making sure you walk in with the advantage already won. About building authority so deep that by the time you shake their hand, the only question left is when you can start.

• • •

The Authority Gap

A truth that will either motivate you or haunt you:

Being good at your job is not enough.

I've watched agents who were exceptional at their craft lose listings to agents half as competent. I've seen the harder worker get passed over for the louder marketer. I've witnessed true specialists lose to generalists who simply showed up more visibly.

It happens constantly. The agent who should have won doesn't. The agent who shouldn't have won does.

Why?

Because competence and perceived competence are two different things. And only one of them gets you hired.

Knowing what you're doing and being perceived as knowing what you're doing are completely different skills. You can master one without mastering the other. Most agents master competence and ignore perception. They assume being good will be enough. They wait for the market to recognize their talent.

The market doesn't work that way.

The market rewards the visible over the capable. Every time.

This isn't a complaint. It's physics. If no one knows you exist, your skills are irrelevant. If no one perceives you as the expert, your expertise doesn't matter. If your authority isn't evident before they meet you, you're starting every conversation from zero.

The authority gap is the space between how good you actually are and how good the market thinks you are. Titans close that gap. They build authority deliberately. They understand that perception shapes reality, and they take control of that perception.

The question isn't whether you're good enough. The question is whether anyone knows.

• • •

The Five Forces of Authority

Authority doesn't happen by accident. It's constructed. Brick by brick. Day by day. Decision by decision.

There are five forces that create it. Neglect any one and the structure weakens. Build all five and you become something rare: the obvious choice in a market full of options.

. . .

Force One: Claim Your Territory

You cannot be the authority everywhere. So you must choose where you'll be the authority.

Territory isn't just geography, though it can be. Territory is whatever domain you choose to own. It can be a neighborhood, a zip code, a school district, a price range. It can be a demographic: first-time buyers, divorcing couples, military families, investors, relocations. It can be a situation: probate sales, luxury properties, new construction, fixer-uppers.

The form doesn't matter. The commitment does.

When you claim a territory, you're making a strategic decision to go deep instead of wide. You're choosing to be known for something specific rather than available for everything general.

There's an old saying: the riches are in the niches. It's a cliché because it's true. Generalists compete with everyone. Specialists compete with almost no one.

Think about it from the client's perspective. When they need heart surgery, they don't call their family doctor. They call a heart surgeon. When someone needs to sell in a specific neighborhood, they don't want someone who "works all over." They want the agent who owns that neighborhood. The one whose name surfaces whenever that area comes up.

Years ago, an agent in my market decided to claim a town as his own. He didn't wait for anyone to crown him the expert. He just started showing up like he owned the place. Within two years, nobody in that town called him by his name. They called him 'Mr.' followed by the town's name, as if there were no other agents in that community. He hadn't asked permission. He'd simply acted like the authority until the town agreed.

The goal isn't to be one of several agents someone might call. The goal is to be the only agent they think of. When someone in your territory hears the word "real estate," your name should surface automatically. Not because you asked them to remember you. Because you made it impossible to forget.

Choose your territory. Then own it completely.

• • •

Force Two: Create, Don't Consume

Most agents are content consumers. They scroll social media. They watch market updates. They read articles about the industry. They absorb, absorb, absorb.

Authorities are content creators. They produce the updates others consume. They write the articles others read. They post the insights others share.

That difference determines everything.

When you create content, three things happen simultaneously. First, you demonstrate expertise. People assume the person teaching knows what they're talking about. Second, you stay top of mind. Regular content keeps your name circulating in places you can't physically be. Third, you build assets that work while you sleep. A video posted today can generate leads three years from now.

Content doesn't have to be complicated. It doesn't require professional production or expensive equipment. It requires consistency and relevance.

What are the questions your clients ask most frequently? Those questions are content. What's happening in your market this week? That's content. What did you learn from your last transaction that could help someone else? Content. What mistake do you see people making over and over? Content.

An agent on my team started doing something simple. Every week, she posts a 'Neighborhood Spotlight', a sixty-second video walking through a different street in her territory, sharing what she loves about it, mentioning a recent sale or two, and ending with one tip for buyers or sellers. It takes her twenty minutes to film and post. But every week, she's reminding her entire network that she knows her territory better than anyone, she's actively working it, and she's a real human being who genuinely cares about the area.

It's not rocket science. It's not viral marketing. It's consistent presence.

If you're teaching, people assume you're the expert. You wouldn't teach something you didn't understand. That assumption, earned through consistent creation, builds authority faster than any credential.

Stop being a consumer. Start being a producer. The people who teach shape the perception of the people who learn.

• • •

Force Three: Get on Stages

Visibility builds authority. But not all visibility is equal.

Being seen at the grocery store is visibility. Being seen on a stage is authority.

When you speak to a group, when you're interviewed on a podcast, when you're quoted in an article, when you're asked to present at a community event, something shifts in how people perceive you. The platform elevates you. The invitation implies credibility. The audience assumes you must know something worth hearing, or you wouldn't be the one talking.

This isn't about ego. It's about physics. The person on the stage is perceived differently than the person in the crowd. Use that physics.

Start small. Speak at a local business group. Present at a first-time homebuyer seminar. Guest on a neighborhood podcast. Get invited to a HOA meeting. Show up on local news when they need a real estate perspective.

One agent on my team started a podcast with a colleague. At first, it seemed like a lot of work for uncertain return. Then something interesting happened. Because they had a podcast, they could approach other podcasters and offer to trade appearances. "We'd love to have you on our show. Would you have us on yours?" Suddenly, they had access to stages they never could have reached alone.

The stage doesn't have to be massive. It has to be relevant. Speaking to thirty people in your target neighborhood is worth more than speaking to three hundred people scattered across the region.

When someone says, "Would you be interested in speaking at..." the answer is yes. Even if you're nervous. Even if it's uncomfortable. Especially if it's uncomfortable. Say yes, figure it out, get on the stage.

The more stages you stand on, the more authority you build. The more authority you build, the more stages find you.

• • •

Force Four: Engineer Social Proof

You saying you're great is marketing. Other people saying you're great is proof.

There's a fundamental difference between the two. Marketing is expected. Everyone markets themselves. Everyone claims to be the best, the most dedicated, the most knowledgeable. The claims blur together into noise.

But when someone else vouches for you? That cuts through.

When a past client tells their friend, "You have to use this agent," that friend is halfway sold before they ever hear your name. When a prospect reads forty five-star reviews before meeting you, the meeting is a formality. When someone watches a video testimonial of a family crying with joy at their closing, the emotional connection is already formed.

Social proof isn't something you hope for. It's something you engineer.

Start with reviews. How many do you have on Google? On Zillow? On Facebook? Now, how many does your top competitor have? If they're beating you, you have work to do. Reviews aren't mysterious. You get them by asking for them, but timing matters. Don't wait until after closing. By then, your clients are buried in boxes, changing addresses, and settling into chaos. The right time to ask is during the transaction, when you're actively delivering value and top of mind. Plant the seed early. Make the request between offer acceptance and closing, when excitement is high but life hasn't yet gotten hectic. Send them the direct link. Follow up if they forget. The agents with the most reviews didn't get luckier clients. They got smarter about when to ask.

Then level up to video testimonials. Written reviews are good. Video is ten times more powerful. There's something about seeing a real person, hearing their voice, watching their body language that creates trust no text can match. Record testimonials at closings. Capture them at your client appreciation events. Even a simple phone video of a happy client is worth more than a polished advertisement.

Don't be shy about asking. Most people are happy to say something nice about someone who helped them. They just need to be asked. The agents drowning in social proof aren't luckier than you. They're more intentional.

Build your proof. Display it everywhere. Let others make the case you can't make for yourself.

• • •

Force Five: Become Inescapable

The final pillar ties the others together. It's about saturation. Presence. Omnipresence.

When someone in your territory can't escape your name, you've arrived.

They drive through the neighborhood and see your sign. They check their mail and see your postcard. They scroll Facebook and see your content. They Google the area and see your name in the results. They ask their neighbor for a recommendation and hear your name. They attend the community 5K and you're sponsoring the water station. They grab a pint at the local brewery and you're on the coaster.

Everywhere they look, there you are.

This isn't about ego. It's about association. When your name appears repeatedly in the context of real estate in a specific area, the brain makes an automatic connection. "This person must be the one to call." They don't even consciously choose you. You become the default.

An agent I know wanted to dominate a specific neighborhood. He didn't just list houses there. He over-promoted every listing he got. More signs. More directionals. More open houses. If a house needed one open house, he held three. Not for the house's sake. For the neighborhood's sake. He wanted everyone driving by to think, "This guy is always doing an open house around here."

They didn't realize it was sometimes the same house. They just registered his constant presence.

He sponsored little league teams. He showed up at every community event. He made sure his business card was on the bulletin board at every local shop. He wasn't just in the market. He was inescapable in the market.

That's the goal. Not to be present. To be unavoidable.

The test is simple: If you called ten random people in your territory and asked, "Who's the real estate agent around here?" how many would say your name? If the answer isn't most of them, you have more building to do.

• • •

The Transformation

When you build authority, something fundamental shifts.

At first, you chase business. You call leads. You pursue prospects. You pitch for listings. You compete for every deal. It's exhausting. Every month starts from zero. Every client must be convinced.

Then authority takes hold. And the game inverts.

The phone starts ringing with people you didn't call. Referrals arrive from sources you forgot you had. Listing presentations feel different because the decision is already leaning your way before you open your mouth. You walk into rooms and people already know who you are.

You stop chasing. They start pursuing.

Commission conversations change. When you have authority, you have pricing power. You're not competing on price because you're not competing at all. You're the obvious choice. The premium you charge reflects the premium value you represent.

Referrals multiply. When you're the known authority, people don't just refer you. They insist on you. "You have to use my agent." The recommendation comes with conviction because your reputation precedes the conversation.

Energy changes. The desperate hustle transforms into confident selection. Instead of wondering where the next deal will come from, you're choosing which deals to take. Your biggest problem becomes deciding who gets access to your limited time.

This is what authority buys you: a business where demand exceeds your capacity. Where people line up for the privilege of working with you. Where your phone rings with opportunities you never created.

The agents who build this aren't lucky. They're deliberate. They built the territory. Created the content. Stood on the stages. Engineered the proof. Became inescapable.

Then they watched the game invert.

• • •

Authority Killers

Building authority takes time. Destroying it happens fast. Avoid these mistakes:

• • •

Trying to be everything to everyone.

The moment you claim every neighborhood, every price point, every client type, you become forgettable. Generalists blend in. Specialists stand out. Choose a territory and commit to it. The fear of missing out on other business is real, but the cost of being nobody's obvious choice is higher.

• • •

Waiting until you have enough experience.

Authority is claimed, not given. No one will tap you on the shoulder and announce that you've earned the right to position yourself as the expert. You claim it by showing up like the expert. By creating content like the expert. By speaking on stages like the expert. Experience helps, but waiting for permission guarantees you'll never get it.

• • •

Creating content once and stopping.

One video doesn't build authority. One post doesn't make you visible. Authority requires consistency over time. The agent who posts every week for a year beats the agent who posts once and waits to see what happens. Frequency beats perfection. Show up regularly, even if the content isn't polished.

• • •

Only showing up when you need business.

People smell desperation. If you only appear in your territory when you're hungry for listings, they'll feel the transaction hunting. Authority is built during the slow seasons, not just the desperate ones. The agent who sponsors the 5K when they're busy earns more trust than the one who suddenly appears when they need a deal.

• • •

Waiting for reviews instead of asking for them.

Happy clients don't automatically leave reviews. They're busy. They forget. They need to be asked. The awkwardness of asking lasts thirty seconds. The absence of social proof lasts until you fix it. Get over the discomfort and build the proof.

• • •

Copying instead of creating.

Your authority must be authentically yours. When you copy another agent's style, voice, or approach, you become a diluted version of them. Find your own angle. Your own voice. Your own way of showing up. The market has room for another authority. It doesn't have room for another copy.

• • •

The Choice

You already have the skills. You already care about your clients. You already do good work.

The question is: Does anyone know?

Authority is the bridge between being great and being known for being great. It's the difference between hoping the market recognizes you and making sure it does.

You can keep competing on a level playing field with every other agent. Keep starting every conversation from zero. Keep proving yourself to people who've never heard of you.

Or you can build the authority that tilts the field in your favor. Claim your territory. Create your content. Stand on stages. Engineer your proof. Become inescapable.

Then watch what happens when you walk into a room where the decision has already been made.

You're not there to convince. You're there to confirm.

That's the authority advantage.

• • •

TITAN TRUTH

The obvious choice was built long before the handshake.

CHAPTER 24

Become the Titan

The Transformation That Was Happening All Along

" You didn't just read a book. You underwent a renovation."

• • •

Stop for a moment.

Before you turn this final page. Before you close this book and return to the noise of your day. Before you add this to the shelf with the others you've read and half-forgotten.

Stop.

Something happened while you were reading.

You probably didn't notice. It wasn't dramatic. There was no single moment where everything shifted. No lightning bolt of insight that changed you instantly. It happened the way all real transformation happens: gradually, then suddenly. One chapter at a time. One principle absorbed after another. One old belief quietly replaced by a new one.

You're not the same person who opened this book.

I don't mean you learned some new techniques. I don't mean you picked up a few scripts you might try. I mean something deeper shifted. The way you see this business. The way you see yourself in it. The way you'll carry yourself when you walk into the next room.

• • •

Part One: The Mirror

The person who picked up this book believed their competition was other agents.

The person holding it now understands the truth: Your competition was never the agent across town. It was never the top producer on the leaderboard. It was never the new team with the flashy marketing. Your real competition was ego, self-doubt, bad habits, and the voice in your head that said you weren't built for this.

That voice is quieter now. You know how to silence it.

• • •

The person who started Chapter 1 measured success by transactions closed.

The person finishing Chapter 24 measures success differently. You understand now that sales is the byproduct, not the goal. Relationships produce transactions. Trust produces closings. Service produces commissions. You stopped selling the day you understood this, and that's precisely when the real selling began.

You lead with serving now. You'll never have to push again.

• • •

The person who highlighted the objection chapter wanted better comebacks.

The person who truly understood it recognizes that objections aren't obstacles. They're invitations. Every "no" is a door. The barrier is never what they say it is. Behind the price objection is a trust gap. Behind the timing objection is a fear. Behind "we're going to think about it" is something they're not saying. You don't overcome objections anymore. You decode them. And once decoded, they dissolve.

You hear what others miss.

• • •

The person who studied Legendary Moments thought they were optional extras.

The person who creates them knows they're the entire game. People don't remember average. They remember moments. The champagne with the handwritten note. The gift that couldn't have come from anyone else. The gesture that proved you saw them as humans, not commission checks. You're not trying to satisfy clients anymore. You're trying to stun them.

Average doesn't live in your vocabulary anymore.

· · ·

The person who read about negotiation wanted to win more arguments.

The person who mastered it understands that negotiations aren't won with arguments. They're won with silence, timing, and emotional composure. Ten percent of conflict is opinion. Ninety percent is delivery and tone. You don't fight harder anymore. You negotiate smarter. You let silence work for you. You stay calm when everyone else is reacting.

Calm is contagious. So is your confidence.

· · ·

The person who discovered The 5 That Decide saw a to-do list.

The person who lives it sees a compass. Lead generation. Appointments. Learning. Follow-up. Networking. Five actions that separate agents who build careers from agents who survive them. You don't wake up wondering what to do anymore. You wake up knowing. The clarity isn't just in your schedule. It's in your identity. You're someone who does these five things whether you feel like it or not, whether the day cooperates or not, whether anyone notices or not.

Discipline isn't punishment. It's freedom. You've tasted it.

· · ·

The person who began this journey feared rejection.

The person completing it has built the calluses. Rejection targets situations, not selves. The wound is real, but the story is optional. You've learned to extract the data and release the emotion. You've developed a reset ritual that prevents accumulation. You don't carry yesterday's rejection into today's calls.

Rejection still lands. But it doesn't stay. That's the difference.

. . .

The person who wondered about authority hoped to be seen as an expert.

The person who builds it understands that authority isn't claimed. It's constructed. Brick by brick. Territorial dominance. Strategic visibility. Content that positions you as the source. Social proof that lets others testify on your behalf. Omnipresence in your chosen arena.

You're not hoping to be chosen anymore. You're becoming the obvious choice.

. . .

Part Two: The Path

You don't need to figure anything out. The path is clear. It's been clear since page one.

Here's where Titans go:

. . .

First, you lock in your territory. You know which one. It crystallized while you were reading. Geographic, demographic, situational. Whatever it is, you own it completely. You stop being one of many and become the only one.

You run the Law of 100. You pick your strategy and you commit. Not until it gets hard. Not until you get bored. One hundred days. The agents who master anything committed longer than the agents who mastered nothing. You already know this. Now you live it.

The 5 That Decide become your operating system. Lead generation. Appointments. Learning. Follow-up. Networking. Every day. Not when you feel like it. Not when the schedule allows. Every day. This isn't what you do. It's who you are.

Your reset ritual is built. When rejection lands, you process it and move. You don't carry it. You don't stack it. You extract the data, release the emotion, and dial again. The agents who last are the ones who've mastered the reset. You're one of them.

You create content. Not because you love cameras or enjoy writing. Because the person who teaches is always perceived as the expert. You become the source, not the consumer. Imperfect is fine. Invisible is not.

• • •

As the weeks pass, momentum builds. You double down on what's working. You abandon what isn't. The Law of 100 reveals the truth, and you act on it.

You engineer social proof. Twenty-five new reviews. Then fifty. Then more than any competitor in your territory. You don't hope for testimonials. You create systems that produce them.

You get visible outside your database. Speaking. Collaborating. Showing up where your expertise can be witnessed by people who don't know you yet. Authority is built in public. You build in public.

The Wheel spins. Every contact, every ten days, no exceptions. The system runs whether you're motivated or not. That's the point. Systems don't require motivation. They replace it.

• • •

Then something shifts. Referrals arrive without asking. Your reputation precedes you into rooms. When you walk into listing presentations, the decision is already leaning your way. Your presentation isn't an audition anymore. It's a confirmation.

You raise your standards. You fire clients who drain you. You say no to deals that compromise your integrity. You've built enough momentum to be selective. The agents who take anyone end up serving no one well. You serve the right people exceptionally.

You mentor someone behind you. Teaching cements mastery. The student's growth sharpens your own.

Your Inner Circle is established. The five seats are filled. You have the mentor who sees ahead, the peer who fights beside you, the accountability partner who keeps you honest, the believer who sees your potential, the student who forces you to stay sharp.

You're no longer becoming. You are.

• • •

Part Three: The Identity

I'm not going to ask you to write anything. I'm not going to give you blanks to fill in or questions to answer. You've done enough work.

Instead, I'm going to tell you who you are now.

What follows is your compass. On the days when rejection stacks up, when the market turns hostile, when the voice in your head gets loud again, return here. Read these out loud. They'll reset your bearing.

• • •

You are someone who controls the controllables.

You don't waste energy on markets you can't influence, competitors you can't control, or circumstances you didn't create. Your response. Your attitude. Your energy. Your discipline. That's your list. Everything else is noise. You hear the noise. You just don't respond to it.

• • •

You are someone who leads with service.

The transaction is a byproduct. You don't chase closings. You build relationships, and closings show up as a result. You've flipped the order that most agents have backward, and it's changed everything. Desperation is gone. Pressure is gone. You simply help people, and they pay you for it.

• • •

You are someone who commits for a hundred days.

Tourists sample. Professionals commit. You don't abandon strategies because they got hard. You don't pivot at the first sign of resistance. You lock in and let time reveal the truth. The hundred days can't be gamed, and neither can you.

• • •

You are someone who earns the first eight seconds.

Your energy is right. Your tone is confident. Your opening hooks rather than apologizes. You sound like someone worth talking to because you know you have something valuable to offer. The telemarketer trap is for other people. Not for you.

. . .

You are someone who hears what isn't being said.

Objections don't stop you. They intrigue you. Behind every "no" is a door, and you've learned to find the key. The barrier is never what they say it is. You decode resistance instead of fighting it, and resistance dissolves when it's understood.

. . .

You are someone who tells stories that sell.

Facts slide off. Your stories stick. You don't convince through argument. You transport through narrative. When you speak, people see themselves in the characters. They feel the outcomes. They make decisions based on emotions your stories evoked.

. . .

You are someone who builds capital, not just transactions.

The closing table is your starting line. Where other agents disappear, you deepen. You understand that one relationship feeds you for life, and you treat your clients accordingly. Your network isn't a list. It's an asset that compounds while you sleep.

• • •

You are someone who creates legendary moments.

Average doesn't live in your vocabulary. You're not trying to satisfy. You're trying to stun. The champagne with the note. The gift they didn't expect. The gesture that proves they're humans to you, not commission checks. People don't remember transactions. They remember moments. You create them.

• • •

You are someone who negotiates without fighting.

Silence is your weapon. Composure is your edge. When everyone else panics, you choose. You don't win arguments. You frame conversations. You understand that ninety percent of conflict is tone, and you control yours.

• • •

You are someone who does the five, every day.

Lead generation. Appointments. Learning. Follow-up. Networking. Not when you feel like it. Not when circumstances cooperate. Every day. Without negotiation. Without exception. This is who you are, not what you do. The distinction matters.

• • •

You are someone whose wheel keeps turning.

No contact left behind. Every ten days, the system touches everyone who matters. You don't rely on memory. You don't hope for luck. You run systems. Systems produce consistency, and consistency produces results.

• • •

You are someone who makes referrals easy.

You don't hint. You don't hope. You engineer. You've made referring you the simplest thing your clients can do, and they do it because you've earned it and made it effortless.

• • •

You are someone who guards their circle.

The five seats are filled with intention. Mentor. Peer. Accountability partner. Believer. Student. You've stopped letting geography or history determine who influences you. You choose. And you protect that choice fiercely.

• • •

You are someone who processes rejection at speed.

The wound lands. The story doesn't. You extract the data and release the emotion. You reset before the next call. Rejection doesn't accumulate in you because you don't let it. The calluses are built. The armor is on.

• • •

You are someone whose authority precedes them.

When you walk into a room, the decision is already leaning your way. You've built it deliberately. Territorial dominance. Strategic visibility. Content that positions. Proof that testifies. You're not one of the choices anymore. You're the obvious choice.

• • •

You are a Titan.

Not because you finished a book. Because of what you became while reading it.

• • •

Part Four: The Welcome

You didn't just finish a book. You joined something bigger.

There are Titans in every market who've walked this same path. Who rewired the same responses. Who built the same systems. Who made the same commitment you're making now.

You'll recognize them when you meet them. They carry themselves differently. They don't chase. They don't beg. They don't discount their worth or apologize for their standards. They've done the work. They've built the calluses. They've earned the authority.

Now, so have you.

• • •

Every Titan has a moment. Not the first closing. Not the biggest commission check. The moment they stopped waiting for permission and started building.

That decision changed everything. Not because the market got easier. Not because the rejections stopped coming. Because they stopped being someone to whom things happened and started being someone who made things happen.

That's the only difference between the agent who survives and the Titan who dominates. Not talent. Not luck. Not timing. The decision to become.

You've made that decision.

I know because you're still reading. The agents who weren't ready put this book down chapters ago. They highlighted a few passages, felt inspired for a day or two, and drifted back to what they were. That's not you. You finished. You absorbed. You're here.

That tells me who you are.

• • •

Some Titans mark this moment.

Not because they need to. The transformation happened regardless of ink on paper. But because there's power in drawing a line. In naming a day. In declaring to yourself that everything before this was preparation, and everything after is execution.

If that resonates:

• • •

THE TITAN'S OATH

I am a Titan.

I lead with service. I commit for the hundred. I do the five.

I build relationships that compound. I create moments that become stories.

I hear what isn't said. I negotiate without fighting. I process rejection at speed.

I am the obvious choice before I walk in the room.

I do not break.

Signature: _____

Date: _____

• • •

If you signed it, you meant it.

If you didn't, that's fine. The transformation happened regardless. The ink is just a marker.

What matters is what you do tomorrow. And the day after. And the thousand days after that.

The path is clear. The identity is yours. Now you prove it.

• • •

TITAN TRUTH

Titan Up.

The 100-Day Titan Challenge

...

This is the proving ground.

One hundred days. Five actions. Every single day.

Complete it, and you'll have done what most agents never will, proved to yourself that your word means something. That when you commit, you deliver. That you have what it takes to build something extraordinary.

Miss a day, you start over.

That's not punishment. That's the point. The challenge isn't the five actions. The challenge is becoming someone who doesn't break promises to themselves.

One hundred days from now, you'll either have proof, or excuses.

Titans don't collect excuses.

• • •

The 5

Five actions. Every day. Non-negotiable.

• • •

1. HUNT

Add 2 new leads to your database every day.

Not names you'll forget. Real leads. Full contact information. People who might need what you offer in the next twelve months.

Two per day. That's it. Some days you'll find them through conversations. Some days through door knocking. Some days they'll come from open houses or events or the person standing behind you in line.

Doesn't matter where. Matters that you find them.

Two leads per day. One hundred days. That's 200 new opportunities in your pipeline that didn't exist before you started.

The hunt never stops.

• • •

2. DIAL

Make 20 phone calls every day.

Not texts. Not emails. Dials.

Twenty times per day, you pick up the phone and call someone. Past clients. Sphere. Leads. Expired listings. FSBOs. Doesn't matter the source. Matters that you dial.

Most won't answer. That's fine. Some will. And those conversations are where your business lives.

Twenty dials per day. One hundred days. That's 2,000 dials. While everyone else is hiding behind email, you're doing the thing that actually works.

The phone is where Titans are forged.

• • •

3. MAKE THE ASK

Ask for 2 appointments every day.

Not hints. Not "let me know if you ever need anything." A direct ask for a specific meeting.

"Can we meet Thursday at 2 to talk about your plans?"

"I'd love to walk through your home and show you what it could sell for. Does Saturday work?"

Two genuine asks. Every day.

Most of your asks will come from your dials. But if you finish your 20 dials and haven't made 2 asks, you're not done.

Get creative. Win the day.

Text someone with a direct ask. Send a handwritten note requesting a meeting. Email with a specific call to action. Make more dials until you get the opportunity.

The rule is simple: Two asks must happen. How you get there is your problem to solve.

Two asks per day. One hundred days. That's 200 times you put yourself on the line. At even a modest conversion rate, that's 20-30 appointments you created from nothing but courage and consistency.

The ask is where amateurs hesitate and Titans advance.

• • •

4. NETWORK

Connect with 1 new person who can expand your world.

Not a lead. A relationship.

A lender. An attorney. A financial advisor. A business owner. A contractor. A fellow agent in a different market. Someone who serves the same clients you do, or knows people you should know, or opens doors you can't open alone.

One new connection per day. A conversation. A coffee. A DM that starts a relationship.

One per day. One hundred days. That's 100 new people in your network who weren't there before. Each one a potential referral source. Each one a node that expands your reach.

Your network is your net worth. Build it intentionally.

• • •

5. TRAIN

Invest 30 minutes in yourself every day.

Time-blocked. Undistracted. Intentional.

This is not scrolling social media and calling it "research." This is deliberate practice. Skill building. Sharpening the blade before battle.

Thirty minutes per day. One hundred days. That's 50 hours of focused training, the equivalent of a full semester college course in sales mastery. While you're working your business, you're also building a credential-level investment in yourself.

What counts:

Scripts and dialogues: practice until they're automatic

Market knowledge: know your numbers cold

Negotiation tactics: study the masters

Mindset and performance: feed your mind

Books, podcasts, courses: learn from those ahead of you

Role-playing with a partner: simulate the pressure

Reviewing your own calls: find the gaps

Shadowing top producers: steal what works

Keep it varied. Stay curious. But stay focused. This is training, not entertainment.

Thirty minutes. Timer set. Phone off. Learn something that makes you better.

. . .

The Math

One hundred days of The 5:

Action	Daily	100 Days
Hunt	2	**200 new leads**
Dial	20	**2,000 calls**
Make the Ask	2	**200 asks**
Network	1	**100 new connections**
Train	30 min	**50 hours (full college course)**

Read that again.

That's not a challenge. That's a career transformation.

And all it costs is a hundred days of keeping your word.

● ● ●

The Rules

No zeroes.

A day with a zero is a day you restart. Back to Day 1. No exceptions.

No banking.

Forty dials today doesn't buy you a skip tomorrow. Each day stands alone.

No excuses.

Sick. Tired. Busy. Traveling. Holidays. Bad days. Hard weeks.

The 5 still get done. Titans find a way. That's what makes them Titans.

Track it.

A calendar. A spreadsheet. A notebook. An app. Doesn't matter how. Matters that you see the streak. Matters that you know your number.

The scoreboard tells the truth.

● ● ●

The Proof

Everyone has goals. Titans have proof.

When you complete the 100-Day Titan Challenge, you'll have something most agents will never have: evidence that you can do hard things consistently.

Not for a week. Not for a month. For one hundred days.

That proof changes how you see yourself. And when you see yourself differently, you show up differently. You carry yourself differently. You perform differently.

The 100 days are the crucible. What emerges on the other side is the Titan.

• • •

You're Not Alone

There are others out there right now, grinding through their hundred days. Fighting the same battles. Keeping the same promises. Becoming the same thing you're becoming.

Post your daily count if you want. Use #MadeTitan so others can find you. Or keep it private, the work matters more than the broadcast.

But when you see another #MadeTitan post, you'll know what it took. You'll know what they're building. You'll know they're one of you.

Iron sharpens iron.

• • •

After the 100

You finished.

You are now a Titan; and you will be for the rest of your life.

This isn't a certificate. It's not a badge someone hands you. It's something no one can give and no one can take away.

It's what you know about yourself.

You know you did the work. Every day. For one hundred days. You know you didn't cut corners. Didn't cheat. Didn't negotiate with yourself when it got hard.

That knowledge changes everything.

The people who skipped days and lied on their tracker? They know too. They'll never feel what you feel; because the title isn't about what others think. It's about what you know.

You know.

• • •

Now your mission changes.

You no longer need someone to tell you what to do next. Titans don't wait for instructions. You've built the muscle. You've proved the identity. You know how to grow, how to push, how to find the next edge.

The 100 days taught you something most people never learn: You'll find your next 100 at the end of the first 100.

There's always another level. Always another edge to sharpen. Always another version of yourself waiting to be built. Titans don't stop expanding. That's not discipline anymore, it's just who you are.

• • •

But here's the final shift:

The first 100 days were for you. The rest are for others.

Find the agent who's struggling. The one who's hungry but lost. The one who reminds you of yourself before you started. Show them the way. Hold them accountable. Help them find the best version of themselves.

Because the person who finishes the Titan 100 is the same person who can build an empire. And empires aren't built alone. They're built by leaders who create other leaders.

You're not just a Titan now.

You're a Titan who makes Titans.

• • •

Day 1

No more waiting. No more "someday." No more perfect conditions.

Day 1 is the Monday after you finish this book.

Circle it. Set the alarm. Tell someone.

And when that morning comes, you don't negotiate. You don't reconsider. You execute.

Hunt. Dial. Make the Ask. Network. Train.

Five actions. One day down. Ninety-nine to go.

• • •

See you at 100.

• • •

#MadeTitan

Continue the Journey

You have the blueprint. Now get the tools.

Visit ThinkSales.com/TOS to access your free Titan Resources:

- The scripts and frameworks from this book

- Tracking templates for The 5 That Decide™

- Video trainings that go deeper on each pillar

- The Titan community—agents who refuse to stay average

The room is waiting.

Acknowledgments

Annie, you've been my biggest fan since before this made sense. You never gave up on the crazy dreams, even when I almost did. None of this exists without you.

To everyone who showed up when it mattered. The early morning huddles. The late night calls. The moments when quitting would have been easier. You didn't. You know who you are. This book is proof that the room works.

To our clients. You trusted us with your homes, your families, and the biggest decisions of your lives. Serving you has been the honor.

And to you, holding this book. You didn't have to pick it up. You didn't have to finish it. You did. Now go prove it was worth it.

www.ingramcontent.com/pod-product-compliance
Lightning Source LLC
Chambersburg PA
CBHW051342280526
45784CB00007B/2785